BAD BOYS

THE LEGENDS OF HOCKEY'S TOUGHEST, MEANEST, MOST-FEARED PLAYERS

STAN FISCHLER

McGraw-Hill Ryerson
Toronto   Montreal

Bad Boys

The Legends of Hockey's Toughest,
Meanest, Most-Feared Players

© 1991 Stan Fischler

First published in 1991 by
McGraw-Hill Ryerson Limited
300 Water Street
Whitby, Ontario
L1N 9B6

Acquisitions Editor: Glen Ellis
Production Editor: Rodney Rawlings
Text Editor: Val Francis

Printed and bound in Canada.

1 2 3 4 5 6 7 8 9 10 AP 0 9 8 7 6 5 4 3 2 1

Canadian Cataloguing in Publication Data

Fischler, Stan, date
   Bad boys : the legends of hockey's toughest,
meanest, most-feared players

Includes index.
ISBN 0-07-551345-5

1. Hockey — Biography.   2. Violence in sports.
3. National Hockey League — Biography.   I. Title.

GV848.5.A1F58 1991   796.962'092'2   C91-094775-9

CONTENTS

I

THE GOOD OLD DAYS OF TOUGH HOCKEY

II

THE ROUGHEST TEAMS

III

INDIVIDUAL ENFORCERS OF THE PAST

IV

THE CONTEMPORARY ERA

V

THE TOUGH GUYS SPEAK OUT

ACKNOWLEDGEMENTS

The author wishes to express his gratitude to those who have been of inestimable help in researching the manuscript and providing anecdotal material and other insights.

For starters, Ira Gitler, who not only is a world-renowned jazz critic and hockey author but also has managed, coached, and played for Gitler's Gorillas. Ira was the first to recognize hard hockey in a literary sense with his book Blood on the Ice.

Many former NHL hard guys delivered significant information. Topping the list was arguably the most intense competitor ever to hit the ice, Larry "The Rock" Zeidel. Not to mention Gordie Howe, who to this viewer's thinking was not only hockey's greatest player but also the toughest superstar who ever came down the pike.

Considerable thanks are in order for the contemporary NHL players who graciously offered their time and thoughts for interviews. It should be noted that some of them did so despite adverse circumstances. Tie Domi of the New York Rangers unhesitatingly agreed to an interview although still grieving over the death of his father. His teammate, Joey Kocur, likewise made himself available although he had been the target of a hostile press after arriving in New York and also was under suspension at the time.

In order to obtain interviews with players in their particular locales, a number of reporters in various cities supplied their time and research. These include Mary McCarthy in Washington, Joel Bergman in Los Angeles, Mike Mouat in Detroit, Michelle Dye in Minnesota, Diane Gerace in Philadelphia, Randy Hu in St. Louis, Linda Lundgren on Long Island, Matt Messina and Lou Villano in New Jersey, and Rita Gelman, Tracy Pattison, and Ashley Scharge in New York.

Thanks should also be given to Matt Messina and Jeff Resnick for their help and dedication as well as Todd Diamond, Eli Polatoff, Juan Martinez, Stuart Kliternick, Mike Blaze, Adrienne Nardo, Teresa Faella, Darwin Lee, Bernard De Sena, Andy Schneider, and Jeff Siegel. And, most importantly, the always-helpful Glen Ellis at McGraw-Hill, as well as good friend Allan Turowetz who helped conceive the project during a walk through Riverside Park.

I

THE GOOD OLD DAYS OF TOUGH HOCKEY

Chapter 1

SANCTIONED SAVAGERY

It was a typical night during the late 1960s in Boston Garden, a funereal arena known to visiting National Hockey League players as the "Zoo." They called it that because, over the years, the home team — the Bruins — had taken a bloodthirsty delight in being known as the "Animals." On this evening they were intent on devouring the Toronto Maple Leafs while more than 15,000 customers played Romans at Caesar's circus. It is the thing to do at Boston Garden as it is in Philadelphia's Spectrum, the Forum in Los Angeles and most hockey arenas up, down, and across North America.

"C'mon, Bobby," a rinkside fan snapped at local folk hero Bobby Orr. "Lessee some blood!"

Before Orr could oblige, Brian Conacher, a tall, husky Toronto forward, found himself on a collision course with Orr. Reacting with the natural self-preservation reflex, Conacher brought his pound-and-a-half white ash stick up to face level. Orr's head lurched back like a man who had just taken a bullet in the stomach. He fell to the ice as blood spurted from his just-broken nose.

Before Conacher could conduct an orderly retreat he was surrounded by the Animals, who mauled him long enough for Orr to clamber to his feet, jump Conacher, and punch the fallen Leaf so ruthlessly that even the partisan Boston *Globe* printed an open letter condemning the brutality.

Orr promptly copped the traditional hockey player's plea — he who sees blood on himself must extract blood from the attacker. "Conacher got me in the nose and I was bleeding like a stuck pig," Orr explained. "I didn't want to fight but if they see you backing out in this league, it's no good."

By contrast, Conacher found the bloodletting too nauseating for his constitution and quit big-league hockey in the prime of his career. In a parting warning, Conacher predicted that such violence for "bloodthirsty American fans" might ultimately destroy hockey.

That was like saying gasoline might ultimately destroy automobiles, or blood might cause arteries to wither. Conacher was unrealistic. Violence has been a part of the woof and warp of hockey since the first game was played in Montreal on March 3, 1875.

As early as 1907, hockey was alternately being denounced and hailed — depending on your metabolism — as the bloodiest of modern games. In a contest that season between Ottawa and Montreal there was so much blood spilled on the ice that the Montreal *Star* headlined it as "an exhibition of butchery."

The official NHL history described the quasi-massacre this way:

> *Baldy Spittal (of Ottawa) was said to have deliberately tried to split Cecil Blachford's skull by bringing down his hockey stick upon it with all his force using both hands. Blachford was carried off with his blood pouring on the ice. Alf Smith was said to have skated across and hit Rod Stuart across the temple with his stick, laying him out like a corpse. Harry Smith was credited with cracking Ernie Johnson across the face with his stick, breaking Johnson's nose.*

Judging by that heartwarming atmosphere, it was hardly surprising that later in that same season a player died as a result of a clubbing he absorbed in a hockey game. The victim was Owen McCourt, a leading scorer on the Cornwall, Ontario team. His crime was getting in the path of a stick wielded by an opponent named Charles Masson.

McCourt was carried off the ice, bleeding from a cut on his head. He died in the hospital the following morning. As a result of the coroner's inquest it was determined that McCourt "came to his death by a blow from a hockey stick."

As for Masson, the report added: "Although there was no evidence of ill-feeling previous to the assault, there was no justification or personal provocation for the blow at the hands of the said Masson.

"After hearing the evidence, your jury recommends that legislation be enacted whereby players or spectators encouraging or engaging in rough or foul play may be severely punished."

But alas, history has demonstrated that such pious suggestions to humanize hockey have melted like the ice in spring. In 1968, Bill Masterton of the Minnesota North Stars cracked his head on the hard, rutted ice and died the next day in the hospital. In 1973 Greg Neeld, a gifted Junior A player took a stick in his right eye and eventually had to have eye surgery. His father correctly assailed hockey "butchery"; several wails were heard from do-gooders and politicians. And less than three months later another teenage boy was beaten up by a rival hockey player and was pronounced dead on arrival at the hospital near Toronto.

Why does a game that combines ballet and bloodshed always seem to accent the crimson? Why have fans literally crashed down doors to see the "Big, Bad Bruins" and the "Ferocious Flyers," while treating the more pacific but more artistic Montreal Canadiens with virtual disdain?

For starters, hockey was invented by Canadians, developed by Canadians, and until recently had been virtually monopolized by Canadians. Despite rumours to the contrary, Canadians have been a hell-for-leather people whose passion for raucousness and the grape was a legend of two world wars.

"Much of the appeal of hockey,"wrote Canadian author Scott Young, "is the combination of blood, sweat and beauty. Perhaps these qualities in juxtaposition have an extra meaning for a nation that is still engaged in pushing back its fierce and beautiful frontiers."

Exposure to bloodshed and death are part of hockey's machismo, which is somehow related to the Canadian psyche. "Hockey reflects us," said the late Lloyd Percival, Canada's physical-fitness expert. "In a game like hockey, you have to have the emotional ability to keep going despite the knocks, without overreacting to the danger."

The roots run deep; from the bitterly frigid outdoor rinks of Canada's Prairie provinces to the comfortable innards of a new, brilliantly lit arena in Toronto. Education of a hockey player begins as early as age three. "Don't fight," a mother tells her preschool son on an outdoor municipal rink in Elmira, Ontario. The boy has discarded stick and mittens to wrestle a friend to the ice. "Don't fight!" she pleads again.

For a split second the lad looks up but only long enough to shout, "But hockey players fight."

They fight because savagery is sanctioned by the NHL. The crash of body against body is legal in many cases and even illegal acts are frequently overlooked by the referees. That, of course, is when the real trouble starts.

Many fans experience a bestial satisfaction — bordering on the sadistic — in totalling the stitches and broken bones of their sworn enemies. Few players have all their own teeth and those who do are regarded as softies.

Gordie Howe, who played 26 years for the Detroit Red Wings and then with the Houston Aeros and New England/Hartford Whalers, would judge a season by goals, assists, and stitches. "I had fifty stitches in my head one year," said Howe. "That was a bad year. I only got ten stitches the following season. That was a good year."

The machismo integrated into the Canadian psyche causes hockey players to virtually dismiss serious injuries. Denis Potvin, the former New York Islanders defenseman, played nearly two months of the 1973–74 season despite a broken leg. Gilles Marotte of the New York Rangers once suffered a broken jaw and leg as well as a nasty thigh cut that took several weeks to heal, but when asked if he had been hurt badly, he shook his head. "No," he said, "I guess I've just been lucky."

They are toughened at an early age. Derek Sanderson's father used to collect his son's hockey stitches in a glass jar. "When I reached a hundred," said Derek, "he threw the bottle away and figured I was tough enough for organized hockey."

The result is adult intensity and stoicism at precocious ages. A Junior C player in Elmira, Ontario, rated highly as an NHL prospect, broke two of his ribs. He went home, spat blood, and waited four days to see a doctor. "If you keep running to a doctor with something minor," he explained, "they don't look at you after that."

Among the young man's souvenirs is a broken nose, never set by a doctor. Urged to wear a protective mask, the young player rebelled with this rationale: "You wear a nose mask and its sets you up as a target. They come after you with high sticks."

Canadians accept the stitches and breaks and scars as matter-of-factly as snow in the winter. "What's so dangerous?" said a Kitchener mother with two sons in organized hockey. "Accidents can happen anywhere."

No athlete underreacts like a hockey player. During a Stanley Cup final, defenseman Bob Baun of Toronto suffered a broken leg. He calmly requested a shot of painkiller from the doctor, returned to the ice, and scored the winning goal in sudden death overtime. Or take the case of Elmer Lach, former star centre of the Montreal Canadiens. Knocked out during a game at Olympia Stadium in Detroit, Lach was carried to the rubbing table in the arena hospital. His face was pale and drawn, and his light, spiky hair was matted wetly across his forehead. A trickle of blood ran out the side of his mouth and down his chin to the white sheet that covered the table, and there it formed a spreading red blot. There was a pervasive fear among the Canadiens that Lach would never lace on skates again.

When the doctor looked down at the victim, Lach winked back. "I can't breathe when I skate because of the blood, is all that's the matter," said the Montreal forward. "I was thinking, maybe if I plugged my mouth with cotton . . ."

Lach's teammate Maurice "Rocket" Richard once was bludgeoned to the ice by Leo Labine of the Boston Bruins during a Stanley Cup series. Lying unconscious in a pool of blood, Richard appeared to be dead. He was finally helped from the ice and revived in the dressing room. Late in the game he quietly returned to the bench and eventually skated through the Boston defense to score the winning goal. After the game, Richard revealed he could not recall a single event from the time Labine hit him to the dressing-room interview.

What obviously makes hockey bloodier than other major sports is the fact that for 60 minutes of playing time each of the 12 players carries a large weapon in his hand — a stick that measures five feet in length and has a pointed tip, the better with which to jab your opponent in the gut.

Some of hockey's more adept infighters claim that the stick is too obvious a weapon to use on a foe, that the referee can easily see it from 30 feet away. They claim it's more practical to use one's skates to separate an enemy from his head along the boards. The razor-sharp

skate blades have a machete-like effect. It has also been discovered
that a swift jab of the skates against an opponent's boot will knock an
opponent right off his feet. Hence the expression "kicking skates."

According to insiders one of the best skate kickers was George "Red"
Sullivan, a peppery centre who played for the Boston Bruins and the
New York Rangers.

It is said that Sullivan made the mistake of kicking the skates of all-
star defenseman Doug Harvey of the Montreal Canadiens. Several
games later Harvey sent Sullivan to the hospital with a stick jab in the
stomach. His explanation was accepted by all who've played big-
league hockey: "He kicked skates! And that's not nice."

Curiously enough, large amounts of blood are not spilled as a result
of the ubiquitous fist fights that occur in hockey games. A noteworthy
exception was a collision in 1951 between "Wild Bill" Ezinicki of the
Boston Bruins and Ted Lindsay of the Detroit Red Wings. When it was
over, Ezinicki required 19 stitches in his head while Lindsay accepted
five. Years later, in a calmer moment, Lindsay offered an insight into
why his and other hockey fights start:

> Ezinicki always liked to give you a last shove. When he
> jostled me I gave it back to him. Then he cut me with his
> stick, and I cut him. We went at it with our fists and I was
> lucky enough to land the best punch I ever threw in hockey.
> It was a right and it landed on the button. After that Ezzie
> kept comin' at me without protecting himself. . . . All that
> started with a couple of shoves.

In more pious moments owners of NHL teams have been known to
condemn the bloodletting, but few observers take them seriously —
any more than one believes a pitchman at a carnival.

Hockey's violence was accepted and encouraged by the owners a
long time ago, and nothing since Conn Smythe was boss of the Toronto
Maple Leafs has changed the prevailing philosophy. Smythe's theme
became a coaching credo: "If you can't beat 'em in the alley, you can't
beat 'em on the ice." Smythe realized, as many other hockey pro-
moters have since, that the prospect of bloodletting lures fans to a rink
like hyenas to a carcass. But every so often, the damage inflicted is so
awesome that even the most savage rooters are stunned to the core.
Just such an episode occurred on December 12, 1933, when Eddie
Shore of Boston charged Toronto's Ace Bailey from behind with so
vicious a blow that Bailey spent two weeks on the critical list and never
played hockey again.

Equally frightening was a one-way decapitation contest conducted
by Bernard "Boom Boom" Geoffrion of the Montreal Canadiens against
Ron Murphy of the Rangers at Madison Square Garden in the early
fifties.

Murphy made the mistake of massaging Geoffrion's face with the side of his stick while they battled along the sideboards. Geoffrion was offended principally because he did not have a stick at the time. Not content with three massages of Geoffrion, Murphy tried for six. Exasperated, Geoffrion finally broke free and found a stick of his own. By this time, Murphy had retreated to centre ice where he suddenly appeared mummified by the oncoming Montrealer. Geoffrion wound up and swung like Hank Aaron going for a grand slam, but he missed Murphy's head by a fraction of an inch. Strike one!

Since Murphy remained firmly — and rather unintelligently — implanted in the same spot, Geoffrion wound up a second time. This time, the full swing of his stick blade cut a wide swath of air and struck Murphy in the jaw, breaking it into many pieces. The Ranger eventually was carted away and years later discussed the phenomenon of hockey stick-swinging. "After the first swing," Murphy said, "you go crazy. All you can think about is trying to protect yourself, and the only way to do it is to get the other guy. When you start swinging, there's no place to run."

Another reason for the frequency of hockey bloodshed is that players expect and accept it as part of their working day. One night, superstar Frank Mahovlich was being mended after colliding with an enemy defenseman's stick. Mahovlich had one red welt about six inches long and the width of a hockey stick across the lower part of his neck, just above the collarbone, and his left shoulder was bleeding in two places from abrasions. Yet he discussed the injuries like a man describing an episode on his front lawn.

"I was getting ready to take a pass when somebody high-sticked me," said Mahovlich. "I saw the stick coming so I pulled my head back, so it got me lower." And that was that.

In August 1974, the National Hockey League was singled out as "the strongest influence contributing to increased violence in amateur hockey in Ontario." The league, with its emphasis on winning and the use of violence as a tactical instrument to achieve that goal, was cited in the report of a provincial government inquiry into the sport conducted by lawyer William McMurtry.

Not long ago, a Quebec judge observed that while homicide was not permitted to go unpunished on the streets of Montreal, everything seemed to be allowed in the hockey rink. "One gets the impression," the judge explained, "that hockey players believe that there will be no police intervention and no criminal charges regardless of what they do on the ice."

To a large extent the judge is right. Ever since Owen McCourt was killed on a hockey rink in 1907, judges have been issuing warnings and hockey players have gotten away with murder — or close to it. Neither judges nor the players themselves really want to legislate against mayhem on skates.

"It's part of the game," said Lorne Henning, now assistant coach of the New York Islanders. "Eliminate it and people just wouldn't pay to see a hockey game."

Perhaps he's right. Violence has been part and parcel of the Canadian and American way of living since the arrival of Columbus. Perhaps hockey's appeal as sanctioned savagery can be understood in terms of a report by the National Commission on the Causes and Prevention of Violence. It helps explain why Americans, in particular, have become more and more infatuated with hockey's bloodshed.

"Our nation was conceived and born in violence," said the report. "In the violence of the Sons of Liberty and the patriots of the American port cities of the 1760s and 1770s.

"The patriot, the humanitarian, the nationalist, the pioneer, the landholder, the farmer and the laborer (and the capitalist) have used violence as a means to a higher end. For all our rhetoric, we have never been a very law-abiding nation, and illegal violence has sometimes been abundantly rewarded."

Chapter 2

HOCKEY'S GREATEST FIGHTS, FROM SHORE TO SHACK

Muzz Patrick, once a defenseman in the National Hockey League, delivered a definitive statement explaining why ice rinks often resemble boxing rings and stickhandlers look more like middleweight challengers than goal scorers.

"Hockey players," said Patrick, "are not paid to fight. They are paid to play hockey." At first one might accuse Patrick of gross hypocrisy. For it was Muzz who was doing on ice what Joe Louis then was accomplishing in the ring. One night Patrick littered the Madison Square Garden ice with the body of Eddie Shore, who until then had been more impregnable than Gibraltar. That was a one-punch operation. On a difficult night, Muzz required two and sometimes three blows to dispatch his foes.

One must read into Patrick's statement for the key to hockey's congenital hostility. Although hockey players are paid to play hockey, they are compelled to become fighters because of circumstances beyond their self-control. These circumstances are a long piece of wood shoved into one's mouth, a knee in the gut or the sharp edge of a skate bayonetting the calf. The frenetic movement of players on a hockey rink suggests two superhighways crossing each other without benefit of traffic lights or policemen. Ergo: collision after collision. Ergo: boiling, then exploding tempers as body meets body at 25 miles per hour on ice.

"Anyone who is surprised at fights breaking out in hockey," observed Scott Young, then an editorial page columnist for the Toronto *Globe and Mail*, "should likewise be surprised each time the sun rises in the east. There is just something about being jammed into the sideboards at high speed, or catching a stick in the face or an elbow in the teeth, which tends to rouse a man's fighting spirit."

Hockey fights conveniently fall into two moulds — individual and Pier Six, with variations on both themes. Sometimes the individual *tête-à-tête* explodes spontaneously, as it did the night Bernie "Boom

Boom" Geoffrion attempted to decapitate rookie Ron Murphy at Madison Square Garden.

Then there's premeditated mayhem. Such as the case when the then Ranger coach Red Sullivan offered to provide a scholarship for Vic Hadfield if the Bunyanesque Rangers' left wing mauled Montreal's Henri Richard in the penalty box at the Forum. Word of Sullivan's antisocial behaviour leaked to NHL President Clarence Campbell, who imposed a heavy fine on Sully.

More often than not, hockey players don't require incentives such as the one Sullivan proposed. The individual grudge fight may be kindled one season and erupt the next. Montreal's elephantine defenseman Ken Reardon remembered that Cal Gardner had dislodged a few of his molars without sedatives when Gardner was a Ranger. Reardon mulled over possible retaliatory gestures for two years and, finally, on New Year's night 1949, Reardon counterattacked with a series of machete-like swings with his stick. Not thoroughly surprised by the offensive, Gardner deflected the blows, whereupon Reardon switched to fist-swinging. Once again, Gardner competently retaliated. The draw cost Gardner $250 and Reardon $200 and each a one-game suspension. Still frustrated, Reardon vowed an escalation of the personal war, and in the March 1950 issue of *Sport* observed that Gardner would be further punished.

NHL President Clarence Campbell read the article and believed that if any punishing would be done, he, Campbell, would do it — to Reardon. The president then issued a $1,000 warning to Reardon: if he attacked Gardner again during his career he would blow the grand. Suddenly, the feud had ended.

As a rule, assassination attempts are not made public. Doug Harvey, a normally reserved Montreal defenseman, nurtured a long hate against the Rangers' Red Sullivan because, Harvey later charged, Sully had a distracting habit of kicking Harvey's skates out from under him during the subtle melees in the corner of the rink. Several times Harvey suggested that Sully reform. But when verbalizing got no results, Harvey jabbed Sullivan in the stomach with the sharp blade end of his stick in November 1956. The Ranger captain crumpled to the ice and was removed to St. Clare's Hospital, where a Catholic priest delivered the last rites. Fortunately, Sullivan recovered, following a spleen operation. A few years later Harvey played defense for the Rangers and Sully was coach. However, insiders contend that the animosity between the two never really abated.

Then there are the tacit, premeditated mass attacks — hockey's versions of gangland's St. Valentine's Day Massacre. It happened most vividly in 1950 during the Stanley Cup semifinal round when Gordie Howe of the Detroit Red Wings suffered a near-fatal concussion after crashing into the sideboards. The Maple Leafs contend it was Howe's fault, that he had charged Toronto's Ted Kennedy, missed, and fell headfirst into the dasher. The Red Wings charged that Kennedy had shoved the butt end of his stick into Howe as he skated by.

By the time the opening face-off approached for the second game of the semifinals on March 30, 1950, a pitch of intense bitterness had been reached. In the Red Wing dressing room players were chanting, "Win this one for Gordie." In the Maple Leaf dressing room there was a grim feeling that the Detroiters were going to try to "get Kennedy." They were right. Midway in the second period Lee Fogolin of the Wings tripped Kennedy. Referee Butch Keeling whistled off Fogolin with a two-minute penalty. As Kennedy got to his feet, Ted Lindsay rushed up and cross-checked him to the ice. Gus Mortson went after Lindsay and then all hell broke loose.

About 20 feet from the Detroit goal, Jim Thomson of the Leafs fell to the ice and Leo Reise bludgeoned him across the head and shoulders with his stick. Defenseless and dazed, the Toronto defenseman reeled from the blows as Reise slashed at his foe until blood flowed down his stick. Having disposed of Thomson, Reise cut across the ice and walloped Kennedy across the back of the neck with his stick.

Lindsay escaped from Mortson's hold and rushed at Kennedy, his stick held high; then Sid Abel broke into the fray, flailing his fists. A fan grabbed Kennedy and manacled him as other Wings struck the Leaf captain. Burdened by 35 pounds of leg pads, Leaf goalie Turk Broda galumphed to the scene to assist his teammate, but Abel and Lindsay continually broke through to poke at Kennedy.

As so often happens in hockey fights, the players' energies dissipated sooner than their hostility. The Red Wing–Maple Leaf battle eventually subsided, only to erupt again in the final minutes of the third period. To some observers it was the worst fight of its kind. "This writer has often vowed that no player would intentionally injure another," said Jim Vipond, then sports editor of Toronto's *Globe and Mail*, "but not after tonight. There could be nothing more brutal and deliberate than the Detroit players' attempt to even a trumped-up injustice to one of their mates."

There was nothing trumped-up about the injustice Bun Cook was trying to even up one March night at Madison Square Garden in the early 1930s. Bun's brother, Bill, was on the receiving end to start with, and if Bun had ever connected he'd probably still be serving out a manslaughter sentence. It happened in a playoff game between the Rangers and the Montreal Canadiens. Bill Cook, the greatest right wing in Ranger history, couldn't untrack himself this night and Nels Crutchfield, a Montreal rookie, wasn't exactly helping him.

First, Crutchfield, who had made the jump to the NHL from McGill University, deposited Cook to the ice with an assortment of checks. Cook, who normally would have gone directly to war with the rookie, stuck to hockey. "I told the referee about it several times," Cook said, "but he wouldn't do anything about it."

Finally Cook cornered the puck and wheeled for a rush toward the

Montreal goal, when who should appear on the horizon but Crutchfield. This time the crafty Cook was ready. He shoved the top of his stick through his gloves and into Crutchfield's body, a routine counterattack. "The next thing I saw," Cook remembered, "was a million stars."

Crutchfield axed Cook across the face with his stick, opening a deep cut.

Cook managed to avert catastrophe by deflecting the assault with his arm but the two blows were enough to defuse him for the moment. "When I finally came around," he said, "all I saw was the stockings of the players who were scrappin'. I never saw so many people getting belted on the ice."

What he didn't see was his brother Bun leading a charge of Rangers over the boards. Bun carried his stick over his shoulder, racing on a collision course with Crutchfield, who didn't see him coming. There are those who insist that Crutchfield would have been dead in less than a minute were it not for a thoughtful gesture on the part of the Cooks' linemate, Frank Boucher, who deftly stuck out his skate and tripped Bun just in front of his intended victim. "Frank told me," Cook added, "that he had to stop my brother or he would have killed Crutchfield."

Just what persuaded the rookie to go on the rampage in the first place baffled observers for many years. It wasn't until 18 years later that Aurel Joliat, Crutchfield's teammate, offered an explanation. "I had dinner with Nels that night," Joliat explained. "Nels ordered a great big steak. They must have given him a side of leather, because he had to saw away at it. After he'd eaten half of it, he made them take it back and bring him another. He ate all of that. I've always figured that meat made him kind of loco."

Cook required eight stitches to close the wound. "I was kinda groggy for the rest of the game." He returned to the lineup in the third period wearing a football helmet. Late in the game he captured the puck, stickhandled through the Canadiens' defense and scored the winning goal. When the series was over, he vaulted the boards and churned his way toward Crutchfield. This time Boucher wasn't around to intervene, but it wasn't necessary. Cook removed his gloves and shook hands with the rookie.

These were the minor classics. They fall short of the all-time plateau because of the severity — or lack of it — of damage in the case of individuals, or the size of the brawls in the mass riots, or the matching of foes. In order to select the ultimate bouts, several interesting ones had to be eliminated. For example, when it comes to mass riots, a decision has to be made between the Montreal–New York game in 1947 as opposed to the Toronto–Chicago brawl a few years later. The latter was conspicuous because of its size but lacked the intensity of individual bouts featured in the Canadiens–Rangers fight.

In the one-on-one category I narrowed it down to Bill Ezinicki vs.

Ted Lindsay, and Lou Fontinato–Gordie Howe. Although the Ezzie–Lindsay fight lasted longer, its implications were less marked than the Fonty–Howe bout. For although Ezzie was cut for 19 stitches to Lindsay's five (a factor Detroit papers erroneously noted as a victory for Lindsay), the Red Wing player carved up Ezinicki, then a Bruin, with his stick, and the fight was hardly as one-sided as depicted by the Detroit partisans. The Howe–Fontinato fight, as you will see, not only spelled the end of a player's image but also exploded his team's playoff chances.

Because this is limited to NHL games, I'm forced to omit what many people have regarded as the bloodiest bout ever: a stick-swinging ruckus between Jack Evans and Larry Zeidel in the Western Hockey League. The players first broke the sticks over each other's bodies; then with splintered wood in their hands continued the bloodbath until the gendarmes intervened.

Eddie Shore–Ace Bailey

Eddie Shore was hockey's Ty Cobb. He was mean, fearless and, above all, a superb athlete. He was the linchpin of the Boston Bruins clubs of the thirties, and certainly its brightest star as the 1933–34 season unfolded. But, somehow, Shore wasn't the old Eddie in the early months of the season and by December he had publicly declared he had to start playing tougher hockey to regain his form.

The night after he made the statement, the Toronto Maple Leafs visited the Boston Garden. Toronto burst into a comfortable lead in a first period that bristled with trouble. At one point Hap Day and Andy Blair of the Leafs were penalized within seconds of each other, compelling Toronto to skate two men short.

The visitor's coach, Dick Irvin, dispatched a penalty-killing trio of King Clancy and Red Horner on defense, and Irvine "Ace" Bailey up front. Under the circumstances, it was an excellent combination. Clancy and Horner were among the best defensive players in the NHL, and Bailey could manipulate the puck as if it were magnetized to the stick. Bailey captured the puck off the face-off and proceeded to bedevil the Bruins with his stickhandling until, finally, the referee blew his whistle ordering another face-off.

Exasperated by the Bruins' futility, Boston coach Art Ross ordered Shore to the bench for a conference. When he returned to the play, Bailey again won the face-off, controlled the puck for several seconds, and then slid it down the ice into the Bruin zone. Shore drifted back for the puck, swerved in his own zone and sped towards the Leaf goal. He rounded the Leaf defense and appeared to be in the clear until Clancy rapped his stick against Shore's skate, temporarily tripping him.

Shore lost the puck and fell to his knees, expecting the referee to call a penalty, which he didn't. Instead, Clancy led a Toronto rush back to Boston territory while Bailey dropped back to Clancy's spot, next to Horner on the blueline. The Leaf players were about 15 feet apart, and if Shore had continued on his course back to the Bruin zone, he would have passed between them. At the time, Frank Selke, then assistant manager of the Leafs, fixed his eyes on Shore from his seat in the press box. Selke vividly remembers the episode.

> About ten feet from the blueline, some unfortunate impulse directed Eddie to change course. Bailey, tired from his exertions, was leaning forward, resting his stick across his knee and watching Clancy battling a couple of Bruins for possession of the puck. Whether he mistook Bailey for Clancy, or whether he was annoyed by his own futility and everything in general, no one will ever know. But we all saw Shore put his head down and rush at top speed. He struck Bailey across the kidneys with his right shoulder with such force that it upended Bailey in a backward somersault while Shore kept on going to his place at the Boston blueline.

The Boston crowd found Bailey's demise amusing but Selke instinctively knew they were confronted by a tragedy of monumental proportions. "We heard a crack you might compare to the sound you remember from boyhood days of cracking a pumpkin with a baseball bat. Bailey was lying on the blueline with his head turned sideways, as though his neck were broken. His knees were raised, legs twitching."

Horner tried to straighten his buddy's neck, but it was locked tight. He noticed Shore and skated to him. "Why the hell did you do that, Eddie?" Shore apparently didn't comprehend the extent of the damage. He smiled.

Livid with fury, Horner drew his right arm back and unleashed an uppercut, striking Shore on the jaw. "It stiffened Shore," said Selke, "like an axed steer."

Boston players emptied their bench like infantrymen going over the top. They made for Horner, but Charlie Conacher of the Leafs vaulted the boards and lined up side by side with Horner, sticks at bayonet position. "Which one of you is going to be the first one to get it?" Conacher challenged, and the Bruins conducted an orderly retreat.

By the time Selke had trotted from the press box to the dressing room, a couple of Bruin fans had attacked Toronto manager Conn Smythe as he was helping carry Bailey to the dressing room. After beating off the attacking fans, the Toronto contingent moved Bailey into the room adjoining the Bruins' clubhouse. "If this boy is a Roman Catholic," the Boston doctor urged, "we should call a priest right away."

At this point Bailey awakened. "Put me back in the game," he wailed. "They need me."

Shore, who suffered a 16-stitch cut in the back of the head, entered the tiny room and approached Bailey, his right arm outstretched. "I'm sorry, Ace," he said, "I didn't mean to hurt you."

Bailey rose from his makeshift stretcher and shook hands. "That's all right, Eddie," the dazed Leaf replied. "It's all part of the game."

Eventually Bailey was removed to a hospital where brain specialists performed surgery for a severe concussion. His condition worsened, whereupon doctors discovered he had suffered a double concussion. A second operation was performed a week after the first one. This time Bailey drifted into a coma. Smythe ordered that arrangements be made to have Bailey's body shipped back to Canada. Meanwhile, a nurse maintained a vigil at Bailey's side. Whenever Ace faded she would wreathe his head in her hands. "Fight," she insisted. "Keep fighting, Ace! The team needs you."

Meanwhile, Bailey's father had taken a train to Boston, a loaded revolver in his pocket. He was determined to kill Shore, and probably would have if a Boston cop hadn't intercepted him in time.

Two weeks later, Ace was released from the hospital and returned to Toronto. He never played hockey again, but he was to face Shore once more. On the night of February 14, 1934, an NHL all-star team played the Maple Leafs, the proceeds going to Bailey. Prior to the opening face-off, Ace Bailey walked out to centre ice and shook hands with Eddie Shore.

Lou Fontinato-Gordie Howe

Devising a formula for checking Gordie Howe was always an obsession with NHL coaches. When Phil Watson coached the Rangers in the late fifties he generally assigned the chore to Eddie Shack. Overpowering and fearless, Shack managed to distract Howe often enough to invite several clouts in the head for his mischief. On this Sunday afternoon, they collided behind the net just as the whistle blew to end play.

It was a rudimentary clash that surely would have been settled in a matter of seconds, except that the balance of power suddenly was disrupted by Lou Fontinato, Shack's teammate. Fontinato, who enjoyed a notorious reputation as the league's bad man and hitherto undefeated heavyweight champion, had a couple of scores to settle with Howe. For one thing, the Detroit superman had nearly sliced Fontinato's ear off with his stick in an earlier game, and for another Fontinato was anxious to erase any doubts about who was the toughest man in the league. Besides, he felt obliged to assist Shack, who seemed to be losing his bout with Howe on points.

Fontinato moved swiftly from his outpost at the blueline. The distance from blueline to the bout was about 70 feet, which the Ranger policeman negotiated in a few seconds. The circumstances were perfect for Fontinato. In most of his fights he would defeat opponents by a surprise attack, raining blows on them before they could muster a defense. Howe, who was concentrating on Shack, didn't see Fontinato coming. The Ranger knocked him off balance and discharged a flurry of punches that normally would have sent an opponent reeling for cover.

But Howe stared down the blows without flinching. He seemed to be sizing up Fontinato. Then the counterattack began. Howe's short jabs moved like locomotive pistons, striking the Ranger around the nose and eyes. *Clop! Clop! Clop!* At about this time the linesman moved in to halt the bout, but nobody wanted to get near the punches. Fontinato returned with a few drives to Howe's midsection but Howe ignored them. The once-feared Ranger was mashed almost beyond recognition. His nose was broken at a right angle to his face, which was dripping with blood. Only one factor saved him from complete disaster — he wasn't knocked down.

The defeat ruined Fontinato. His air of braggadocio vanished. His play deteriorated and so did the Rangers. Coach Watson traced the team's amazing end-of-season collapse and last-day ouster from a playoff berth to the Fontinato disaster. Fontinato eventually was traded to the Canadiens, where his career abruptly ended when Vic Hadfield of the Rangers crashed him into the boards of the Montreal Forum, breaking his neck. Fontinato never played hockey again.

The Richard Riot, 1955

There is absolutely no doubt that the supreme hockey eruption — and one that almost surely will never be equalled — was the one euphemistically known as "the Richard Riot of 1955."

It actually flamed on March 13, 1955 in Boston Garden as a major brushfire, but by the time action had shifted to Montreal later in the week, the brushfire set in motion a series of explosions heard round the world. A day after the riot had officially ended, a Dutch newspaper reported that 27 persons had been killed as a result of the disturbance, which, while untrue, at least indicates the magnitude of the interest.

Maurice "Rocket" Richard, *l'enfant terrible* of the Montreal Canadiens, then the most prolific scorer in hockey, and most hot-tempered of the fiery Flying Frenchmen, was enjoying the most successful season of his long career. Always a high goal-scorer, this year it also appeared that the Rocket would collect enough assists to win his first scoring championship.

Although closely pursued by the Detroit Red Wings, the Canadiens led the league in the home stretch and appeared as capable of finishing first as Richard appeared sure to win the scoring race. But the volatile Rocket had been hounded by opposing checkers — normally inferior players whose only ability was wood-chopping at Richard's heels — and already had been on the carpet for clouting referee Red Storey during a game with Toronto.

Once again the diffident, unobtrusive Hal Laycoe, who figured so prominently in the 1947 Montreal–New York riot and helped trigger the Reardon–Gardner uproar, was to incite the Richard ruckus. It happened late in the game. Boston led 4–2, with six minutes remaining. A penalty left the Bruins one man short. In a desperate attempt to get a quick goal, Montreal coach Dick Irvin removed his goalie and sent six men onto the ice.

Richard was gliding over the Boston blueline when, without warning, Laycoe's stick sliced open a bloody gash on the left side of his head. Referee Frank Udvari signalled a delayed penalty to the Bruin because Montreal retained possession of the puck. When the whistle blew, Richard returned to the blueline. He put his hand to his head and realized it was spurting blood. He also realized Laycoe was eligible for a five-minute major penalty for drawing blood, instead of a two-minute minor, but Udvari didn't change his decision.

Richard flipped. He skated over to Laycoe, who was a short distance away. Lifting his stick high over his head with both hands, Richard smashed Laycoe over the face and shoulders with all his strength. Somehow Laycoe weathered the blows, dropped his gloves, and suggested that they fight it out with bare fists.

Precisely at that moment, Cliff Thompson, a linesman and former Boston Bruin defenseman, rushed Richard and yanked the stick away from the mercurial Canadien. But Richard was like a crazed bull. He unshackled himself from Thompson, found a stick, and slashed Laycoe until the wood cracked. Undaunted, Thompson cornered Richard, but only momentarily. Richard found another stick and belaboured Laycoe until Thompson rushed in and pulled Richard to the ice.

The Rocket still had not been defused. A teammate helped him to his feet. He gazed around, found Thompson and leaped at the linesman, raining blows until Thompson backed off with a black eye and bruised face, then returned to herd the exhausted Richard toward the first-aid room.

Richard, of course, was tossed out of the game and within hours demands echoed across the United States that he be severely punished. "If Richard is permitted to play one more game this season," wrote Detroit writer Marshall Dann, "Campbell should be fired."

On March 16, Campbell held a three-hour private hearing surrounded by Richard, Irvin, Ken Reardon, by now a Canadien executive, referee-in-chief Carl Voss, referee Udvari, linesmen

Thompson and Sammy Babcock, Laycoe, and Lynn Patrick, manager-coach of the Bruins. "I don't remember what happened," Richard said. Then he later added: "When I'm hit I get mad and I don't know what I do."

The hearing ended and Campbell deliberated privately for more than three hours before announcing his decision. "Richard is suspended from playing in the remaining league and playoff games."

News of the suspension sliced right through to the nerve of Montreal. Driving toward a grade crossing, a bus driver was so upset by the decision he ignored a warning signal and barely evaded an oncoming train. An official of the Russian embassy blamed the suspension on the English and Americans. The NHL office was assailed by phone calls. "Tell Campbell I'm an undertaker and he'll be needing me in a few days," warned one fan. "I intend to kill you," cried another, "and I already have a hiding place picked out."

If Campbell had remained incognito he likely would have been secure. NHL business could have taken him out of Montreal without hesitation. At worst, he could have holed up at a friend's house until the fury had subsided. Instead, he headed straight for his enemies.

On March 17, the day after his decision, the Canadiens were to play the Detroit Red Wings at the Forum. The Wings had climbed right behind Montreal in the standings, which only added to the fans' resentment. By game time, the arena was surrounded by a seething mob of 600 demonstrators, many carrying signs saying "Vive Richard" and "À Bas Campbell." When the Forum loudspeaker announced all seats were sold a picketer yelled back, "We don't want seats. We want Campbell."

They were soon to get him. Despite pleas that he remain home, Campbell drove to the rink minutes after the opening face-off. He was accompanied by his secretary and her sister. Somehow, Campbell entered the Forum unnoticed and reached his seat without incident. In a trice, the fans spotted him and unleashed a fearsome roar, "Shoo Campbell, shoo Campbell. . . . Va t'en, va t'en," through the period, which ended with Detroit leading 4–1.

The cascading hoots soon were followed by volley upon volley of vegetables, eggs, tomatoes, rubbers, bottles, and programs. "Go home, please go home," a fan urged Campbell. The president was resolute. "I tried to avoid doing anything that would provoke the crowd," he said later, but even the act of wiping garbage off his face infuriated them to greater assaults. A fan bluffed his way past an usher and socked Campbell several times before other ushers dragged him off.

"This is a disgrace," said Maurice Richard, who was sitting in a seat near the ice with Canadiens' physiotherapist Bill Head.

Instead of heading for cover during the intermission, Campbell remained in his seat. Soon an angry mob descended from the upper seats and menacingly surrounded him. It was 9:11 p.m. and Miss

Phyllis King, Campbell's secretary, believed they were moving in for the kill. The police were not there to protect him. They had been summoned outside to control the mob that was swelling outside the building.

At this moment of imminent doom Campbell was delivered to safety by an unidentified fan who undoubtedly had no intentions of helping him.

A bomb hurtled through the air, exploding about 25 feet from Campbell. Tear gas burst from its seams, fanning out in an ever-growing cloud over the grandstands. Women screamed. Men cried and choked. A cry of "Fire!" went up and 14,000 fans stumbled to the exits. A disastrous panic was avoided when police director Tom Leggett assigned his men outside the Forum to keep the exits open.

Campbell, who was momentarily forgotten, escaped to the first-aid room, 50 feet from his seat. Richard groped his way to another first-aid room, lamenting the disaster. "This is terrible, awful," he said. "People might have been killed." Armand Paré, head of the Montreal fire department, refused to permit the game to continue and ordered the Forum closed. Campbell agreed and forfeited the game to the Red Wings.

When the gasping, angry fans reached the streets outside the Forum they were greeted by hundreds of demonstrators. The groups fused into a maniacal force of thousands. "It seemed," said Frank Selke, "as if an angry sky had suddenly fallen on the city. Hoodlums were swooping in every direction, smashing shop windows, pelting trams with bottles and chunks of ice, and setting bonfires in the streets, jostling with police and looting."

Radio station CKVL had been providing a crash-by-crash description of the chaos that only inspired the curious to venture downtown. By 11:00 p.m. more than 10,000 Montrealers and 200 police were involved in the pandemonium. The Forum was under siege.

Wrestling promoter Eddie Quinn was holed up in his Forum office with a friend. "Nobody will bother us here," Quinn insisted. "Everybody knows I'm a Richard fan." Within seconds a huge rock smashed through Quinn's window.

Richard and his wife unobtrusively left the Forum at 11:15 p.m. by a back entrance. Campbell did likewise at 11:30, guarded by a huge cop. Jim Hunter, the Forum building superintendent, drove Campbell and Miss King home. "I had a fine night's sleep," Campbell said.

Unknown to Campbell, the crowd's fervour had lost all proportion. A mob set fire to a newsstand. Another group smashed windows along Ste-Catherine Street, Montreal's main drag, destroying more than 50 stores for a total of $100,000 in damages.

The riot petered out at 3:00 a.m. Police had arrested 70 people, 27 of whom were under eighteen. Montreal's hangover was severe. "I am ashamed of my city," wrote Dink Carroll in the *Gazette*. Richard returned to the Forum to deliver a public statement over radio and television. "So that no further harm will be done," he said, "I would like to ask everyone to get behind the team and help the boys win from the Rangers and Detroit. I will take my punishment and come back next year to help the club and younger players to win the Cup."

Without Richard the Canadiens were beaten out for first place by the Red Wings and were eliminated in the Stanley Cup finals four games to three. Bernie "Boom Boom" Geoffrion won the scoring championship Richard had coveted so dearly, beating out the Rocket by a single point.

The Rocket vowed he'd come back and he did. He never won the scoring championship but, avoiding trouble, he returned the following season to lead the Canadiens to first place and the first of five straight Stanley Cups.

Chapter 3

HOCKEY'S SINGLE GREATEST FIGHT

I swung my stick at him and missed.
Then
a cop grabbed me from behind and I fell.

There are endless debates over which was the greatest hockey fight of all time. Some will say Eddie Shore–Ace Bailey and its aftermath while others will cite some of the Dave Schultz Broad Street Bullies' battles.

In the author's opinion, the NHL's supreme battle royal took place in New York late in the 1946–47 season. Its chief protagonists were Ken Reardon of the Montreal Canadiens and Cal Gardner of the New York Rangers. But actually it involved just about every player on both teams.

To understand the roots of the riot, one must first examine the players. Gardner was a brash newcomer to the league who was establishing himself as a tough man with his fists and his stick. His opponent was a bit more experienced.

Reardon was ruggedly handsome but unpolished when he joined the Canadiens in 1940–41. He started modestly with 41 penalty minutes in 46 games but was hit for 83 in only 41 the following season before going off to war — the other kind.

His partner, on his return in 1945–46, was Butch Bouchard, another rough-cut gem who had become one of the league's best during Kenny's absence. Butch's presence alone was enough to discourage enemy bullies from getting ideas.

Reardon was wilder and flakier. Above all, Reardon was a competitor who had courage by the carload. He also had a Gaelic temper. I remember a rinkside fan raining profanity on him one night at Madison Square Garden during a "break in the action," as they say on television. Reardon took his gloves off, reached down and grabbed a handful of snow-ice. Then he reached over the protective glass and anointed the guy.

Once at Chicago Stadium a fan yelled at Kenny, "You're a brave man with a hockey stick in your hand." The way it's been told, Reardon reached over with that same stick and opened up the man's head. Leo "Tiger" Gravelle and Billy Reay skated over to help their teammate. A fan jumped on the ice, but referee Chadwick repulsed this invasion. Others pressed up against the outside of the boards but were prevented from spilling onto the rink's surface by the ushers.

Charges of assault were brought against Reardon, Gravelle, and Reay by four members of the crowd, and the three Canadiens were arrested at the end of the game. Blackhawk president Bill Tobin had to post bonds in order to prevent the trio from spending the night in jail. That, however, was small stuff compared to the NHL's royal brawl.

On March 16, 1947, a week before the season's end, Ken Reardon was carrying the puck in the last minute of a game against the Rangers at Madison Square Garden. The Canadiens led 4–3, and Reardon wasn't about to give up the puck. On his last visit to New York he had lost the puck and the game, and coach Irvin had been livid.

The previous night Montreal had edged the Rangers 1–0 at the Forum. The Habs were close to clinching first; the Rangers were facing mathematical elimination from a playoff berth. There had been some bad feeling in that close contest, but things were even hotter at the Garden. In the second period Reardon and Maurice Richard became entangled with Bill Juzda and Bryan Hextall. Irvin later was to charge, "They were out to get Richard and Reardon in order to ruin them for the playoffs. We already had killed the Rangers' chances for the play-offs so they wanted revenge."

"Keep your head up," is the first thing a coach tells the novice player, but it's a lesson most participants have to learn the hard way, nevertheless. Reardon knew better, but he took more than a quick peek at the round object he was cradling at the end of his stick. While he was thus engaged, Bryan Hextall, the Rangers' hard-rock winger, laid a hip into Kenny. As he bounced off Hextall, his face ran into the stick of Cal Gardner. "My upper lip," says Reardon, "felt as if it had been sawed off my face."

After being revived by Doc Nardiello, the Rangers' physician, Reardon skated off for some stitch work. To do this he had to pass the Ranger bench. First he was heckled by the Rangers, led by Phil Watson. Then a fan joined in the verbal abuse. "I've been waiting a long time for you to get it, you louse," he cried.

Kenny, who had punched a Garden patron in 1946, was in no mood to be baited as his mouth continued to bleed painfully. He swung his stick at his balding insulter and missed. Then several of the Garden's special police grabbed him from behind and down he went. From the

Canadiens' bench, across the ice, it appeared that Reardon was about to be victimized by a horde of Blueshirts. The Frenchmen flew over the boards across the ice. When they saw that the Rangers had not attacked their mate, they began worrying a few fans.

With goalie Durnan using his big stick to cut up the air, they invaded the narrow corridor, just past the Ranger bench, that led to the first-aid room. Butch Bouchard argued with the bald fan and then applied a stick to his shiny dome. Durnan and Richard began tussling with other paying customers, and this aroused the Rangers to repel the invaders. They forced the Canadiens to relinquish their beachhead, and fighting commenced in earnest as it spilled back onto the ice.

Opponents squared off, and at the outset they lined up as follows: Richard vs. Juzda; Durnan vs. Bill Moe; Leo Lamoureux vs. Hal Laycoe; and Bouchard vs. Hextall. Moe–Durnan and Lamoureux–Laycoe were boxing bouts; the others were no holds barred.

Moe decked Durnan with a roundhouse right. Laycoe and Lamoureux slugged toe-to-toe until arm weariness forced them to quit. Meanwhile, Richard had slammed Juzda so hard over the head that his stick snapped, but "the Beast," as the Ranger defenseman was known, rose like a stegosaurus from some primeval ooze and slammed Richard to the ice. Bouchard succeeded in wrenching Hextall's stick from him and then floored him with one punch. Moe came to the rescue and broke a stick on Bouchard's skull. Butch acted as if nothing had happened.

Another Ranger defenseman, Joe Cooper, ducked a dangerous Murph Chamberlain haymaker and countered with a stiff right that deposited the Montrealer in a side promenade seat. Juzda left Richard, picked up a loose stick, and broke Buddy O'Connor's cheekbone.

The carnival of swing and swat lasted 20 minutes as it ebbed and flowed all over the Garden ice. At its height 15 fights were going on. Eight special cops were helpless in the face of it, and when organist Gladys Goodding began "The Star-Spangled Banner," it was treated as background music for the hit parade.

There were two noncombatants on the ice. Phil Watson, of all people, and George Allen, who had been teammates on the Rangers in 1938–39, agreed to stand this one out. Watson took Allen aside and said, "What's the sense of getting all tangled up?" Allen said okay. "It was the best fight we ever saw," says Phil.

In an amazing show of lenience, or bewilderment, referee George Hayes gave only three penalties, ten-minute misconducts to Richard, Juzda, and Chamberlain. As a thank-you, Tony Leswick tried to run a stick through Durnan, while the normally peaceful Ab DeMarco skirmished with Ken Mosdell, all in the last 30 seconds. At the buzzer, the police quickly made sure that the teams went to their dressing rooms on opposite sides of the rink.

The bald spectator took three stitches. Reardon needed 14. On the train back to Montreal he grumbled, "I was the guy who started the damn fight, but, believe it or not, I never saw it. Right after the cop knocked me down, I got up and walked to the clinic. I didn't find out about the fight until the game was over, and the guys came into the bloody room all cut. Sorta burns me up. I coulda had a great time."

As weeks passed he thought less about a "great time" and more about who had battered his mouth. He had thought it was Hextall, but when Laycoe was traded to the Canadiens he informed Kenny that it was indeed Gardner. A year after the initial incident, the two collided and Gardner sustained a broken jaw in two places. Not many who were there thought it accidental. The following season, 1948–49, Cal was traded to Toronto.

On January 1, 1949, at Maple Leaf Gardens, Reardon and Gardner engaged in what George Hayes called "one of the wildest stick-swinging duels I have ever seen." Referee Chadwick had given both men slashing minors, and things seemed to have calmed down from a brief, but potentially inflammatory, altercation. Then Gardner said something to Reardon, and when Kenny turned around to confront him, he saw that Cal's stick was high once more. He quickly accepted the challenge, and while linesman Hayes tried to separate them, they flailed away at each other's head and shoulders. Next they dropped their wooden weapons and began throwing fists in a match described as a "life-and-death grapple." Gardner was fined $250; Reardon $200.

In February 1950, a month after Reardon had been fined $25 for a fight with Ranger Pentti Lund, an article co-authored by Reardon and Montreal sportswriter Vince Lunny appeared in Sport. It aired Kenny's version of the 1949 stick-swinging episode and spelled out his future plans for Gardner.

"Someday," Lunny wrote, "the Canadiens' wild Irishman is going to carve Gardner into little pieces, and it will take a brave man to restrain him."

Lunny also described Reardon as a man "who intends to pursue his course of intended action even at the risk of being expelled from the league."

Reardon threatened, "I am going to see that Gardner gets 14 stitches in his mouth. I may have to wait a long time, but I'm patient. Even if I have to wait until the last game I ever play, Gardner is going to get it good and plenty."

Upon reading the article, president Clarence Campbell said Reardon would have to post a $1,000 cash bond with the league "for his good conduct in the future" and further decreed that he would be "entitled to petition for its refund when he retires from the league." Campbell stated that he believed Reardon had meant it when he told him that he no longer intended to pursue the feud.

The regular season ended without any further trouble between Gardner and Reardon. In the playoffs, the Canadiens faced the Rangers at Madison Square Garden. The series went without incident. Although Reardon was voted to the first All-Star team, a chronic back condition forced him to retire before the 1950–51 season. He got his $1,000 back and moved into a vice-presidency with the Canadiens.

Although many intense feuds are healed by time, this was not the case with Reardon and Gardner, who loathed each other decades after the battles.

Chapter 4

A POTPOURRI OF PUCK PUNCHING

Hockey turbulence — meaning fist fights, stick battles, and other forms of mayhem — takes on so many forms that it is often impossible to categorize them. There have been classic incidents which involve long-term grudges and other which were spur-of-the-moment heavyweight bouts (John Mariucci vs. Jack Stewart) that were more noteworthy for their viciousness than their longevity.

Herewith is a potpourri of puck punch-outs covering several decades.

The Flames Debut in Atlanta

In October 1972 ice hockey came to Atlanta, Georgia. Although the residents of Peachtree Street may once have thought a cross-check was a way of monitoring the activities of the Ku Klux Klan and the term left winger may have scared them a bit, the freshly lit Flames caught on at the Omni. The management had chosen judiciously in the expansion draft, and the colourful French-Canadian coach Bernard "Boom Boom" Geoffrion was doing a splendid job with players and fans alike, on and off the ice. But it wasn't until January 19, 1973, that they became rebelliously revved up. The opposition was the St. Louis Blues, a team not known for its gentle approach. The game was in the third period.

On the Blues defense was one Harry Steven Durbano, holder of numerous penalty records in the minor leagues and already well on his way toward adding to this reputation in the majors. Returning from a bout with mononucleosis, Durbano showed none of the usual after-effects when he skated through the Atlanta goal crease. Steve not only violated this sacred ice space but barged directly into Phil Myre, the Flames' goalkeeper, removing him from the crease and taking him off his feet.

Now it is common knowledge that when a skater of the opposing team gets too close to the crease, goalies have been known to use their large sticks to discourage these intrepids from repeating the manoeuvre, by giving them what is affectionately called a "two-hander" (a blow delivered with the hockey stick held in both hands) in the very vulnerable area of the opponent's ankles. Many a player has been severely bruised or has even suffered a cracked bone in the process. Since Myre was falling at the time, he didn't go for the ankles. Instead he reached up and out and belted Durbano in the back of the head, opening a small cut. "He pushed me out of the crease while a shot was being taken," said Myre, "and I had to show him he couldn't get away with that."

Durbano countered, "I didn't come in to take him out, but I banged into him. He must have been off balance when he hit me because he didn't do much damage. But I was really angry because he clubbed me. You don't just do that — hit a guy in the head from behind with your stick."

Appropriately incensed, Durbano charged the goalie, but burly Bob Paradise, an Atlanta defenseman, intercepted him and held him off. St. Louis trainer Tommy Woodcock started to take Durbano to the dressing room, but when Steve heard that the head wound would only require a couple of stitches, he told Woodcock that he could sew him up after the game, and headed for the penalty box. On the way he decided to make a stop. "Myre was standing all alone at his net," explained Durbano, "and I figured I may as well get him now because I might not get another chance."

Durbano proceeded to jump Myre from behind, setting off what has been described as the bloodiest brawl in Atlanta sports history. Both benches emptied, and brawling commenced all over the ice and continued for about a half hour. Even the backup goalies, the Flames' Dan Bouchard and the Blues' Bob Johnson, went at each other until Atlanta forward Billy MacMillan dispatched Johnson with a bloody face.

Hockey News correspondent Jim Huber described the audience reaction.

> *How did the socially conscious Atlanta crowd take it? Did they cover their eyes in horror and stalk out in disgust? Did they summon the police, order the game outlawed? Hardly.*
>
> *Within moments, there were 15,078 screaming people on their feet, pushing so close to the fight that they had to be warned not to lean on the glass, screaming their lungs out, throwing beer, pretzels, programs, and anything that wasn't screwed down.*

In other words, Atlanta fans had reached a parity with their counterparts in New York, Boston, Philadelphia, etc., before the completion of their first season.

Huber wrote: "Flame officials privately saw the brawl not as a half-hour interruption of an excellent hockey game but as money in the bank. They began predicting sellouts for the remainder of the season, and the way the fans attacked the ticket agencies the next morning, their predictions appeared to have been coming true."

Foes to Friends

This is the case of defenseman Ed Van Impe and forward Claude Laforge. While playing against each other in the American Hockey League, Van Impe went into the boards headfirst, courtesy of Laforge. Later in the season he wreaked his revenge. Laforge's jaw was broken, and nine teeth were permanently separated from his gums. When he came to, he vowed to get Van Impe "if it's the last thing I do in hockey."

This was related to Van Impe by a third party. Unperturbed, Ed responded with, "That S.O.B. could have broken my neck when he put me into the boards. Too bad I didn't kill him."

Several years later the two men became teammates on the first version of the Philadelphia Flyers. Soon they were buddies. "It may have seemed funny to outsiders, but not many hockey players hold grudges against each other," said Van Impe. Then the two went out for a drink, with big Ed springing.

How about this one. In November 1972, Garry Unger of the St. Louis Blues, known more as a scorer than a hatchetman, skated a long way to get Ab DeMarco of the Rangers from behind with an upward movement of his stick and then cross-checked him in the back for good measure. DeMarco slumped to the ice and was taken to a St. Louis hospital.

The next day DeMarco had a visitor. It was Unger, his would-be assassin, who gave him two books and expressed the hope that "it wouldn't be too serious."

When Emile Francis heard this, he said wryly, "Maybe someday when Unger comes to New York, DeMarco will visit *him* in the hospital."

On Unger's next New York appearance, the fans at Madison Square Garden booed him whenever he touched the puck, but no one came close to putting him in the hospital. In a later game, he and DeMarco took the gloves off for a short spat. Ab, a peaceful type, felt that this ended the feud. His revenge was minuscule.

Ironically, toward the end of the same season, DeMarco was traded to St. Louis. Soon his best friend *and* roommate was — you guessed it — Garry Unger.

Jimmy Orlando vs. Gaye Stewart

During the first season of the six-team league (1942–43) Toronto's nineteen-year-old rookie left wing Gaye Stewart was formally introduced to Jimmy Orlando, the swarthy veteran of the Detroit defense.

"You're pretty fresh for a rookie," is the way Jimmy supposedly began the niceties. The mouth uttering this challenge was set in a face whose blue-gray stubble would have made Orlando a natural for Gillette commercials had he lasted until the coming of television.

"Why don't you get yourself a shave?" was Stewart's reported retort.

This was followed by a left that began at Orlando's knees and ended on Stewart's jaw, putting his light out. When the Leaf's head cleared he played with renewed vigour, carrying the attack to the Red Wings. Gaye blew down the left side on one of these rushes, controlling the puck until Jimmy loomed in front of him. He then rejected the puck as the object of his stick's affection and replaced it with Orlando's head. The pole-axing of Jimmy's skull prompted Canadian writer Jim Coleman to reflect: "The only time I saw more blood was the day I was taken on a tour of the cattle-killing floor of an abattoir."

Elmer Lach

Lach eventually was to gain stardom as the centre of Montreal's famed Punch Line with Rocket Richard and Toe Blake on his wings. He might have shone for the Leafs, but Conn Smythe insulted him by impugning his size in Toronto's training camp. When he packed his bag and headed for Montreal, Dick Irvin, in his first season as Canadiens' coach after leaving the Leafs, made good use of him. Lach proved to be a lot tougher than Smythe had envisioned, but in an early encounter with Earl Seibert, the dreadnought of the Blackhawk defense, he didn't fare too well.

On his first excursion into the Chicago zone he gave Seibert a stick across the eye. He got off with a warning, but it went unheeded, for in the next period he worked on the area over Earl's eye once more. This time he received a threat that became reality in the final period when Elmer made the mistake of watching the puck as he carried over Chicago's blueline. Seibert hit him with his 200 pounds, albeit legally, and Lach did not play again for three months.

In Lach's second year, 1941–42, the Canadiens opened at home against the Red Wings. They lost the game, 3–2, and Lach, too, when he crashed into the boards and broke his elbow. It was his first and last game of the season.

In the opening game of the 1949 playoffs, Lach's jaw was broken in a collision with "Black Jack" Stewart of Detroit. The Canadiens claimed Stewart had done it deliberately, but the Wings vigorously denied any wrongdoing.

"Elmer doesn't carry the puck in his teeth," reasoned Dick Irvin, "but that's where they've been checking him."

Lach announced his retirement but didn't follow through.

Rocket Richard, the hockey immortal who played alongside Lach for many years, put Elmer's attitude into focus. "He suffered a lot of injuries during his career," explained Richard, "some of which were caused by deliberate efforts to injure him on the part of our opponents. Having played with Elmer for so long, I can appreciate how he might antagonize another player. On the ice, Lach was the kind of guy who used to get the other players mad with some trick or other. He would tease them by hooking or holding, but he never wanted to fight. All he wanted to do was to get the others angry."

Lach got more than he wanted. One of his more severe injuries occurred in February 1947. Toronto winger Don Metz checked Elmer, and when the large-nosed Canadien centre landed on the ice with great impact, he fractured his skull. Metz was given a two-minute penalty but claimed, at the time, that it was a perfectly legal hit. "I struck Lach from his side," said Metz, "but did not see him fall." His boss, Conn Smythe, also was vehement in his insistence that Lach had not been the victim of foul play.

Montreal, however, wasn't buying any Leaf explanations. Baz O'Meara, in the *Star*, wrote: ". . . a ridiculous minor penalty for what probably was intended to be a charge, if not, indeed, a planned effort to put Lach out of action."

Dink Carroll observed in the *Gazette*: "The way we saw it, and the way 90 percent of the people we have discussed it with saw it, he (Lach) was 'speared.' Don Metz tore into him from the side and knocked him heavily on the ice. Elmer never saw Metz, and it was entirely unexpected."

Black Jack Stewart

The Detroit defenseman accumulated 50 scars and 220 stitches but never missed a minute because of it during his first ten years in the NHL. "Sew fast, Doc," he would say. "I'm due back on the ice." He was insured for $100 a season with a policy that paid him back $5 a stitch. He once played an entire season with a broken hand. A special device attached to his stick and wrist enabled him to firm up his grip.

Jack Adams called him "one of the strongest guys I've ever seen in a hockey uniform. He worked hard on his farm all summer and that probably accounted for it."

When Stewart came out of the RCAF after World War II, he had a wheat farm in his birthplace of Pilot Mound, Manitoba. Ted Lindsay remembers:

> When Jack came to training camp, he was in better shape than when he went home in the spring. He was the toughest man I ever faced.

He was a mean individual, but generally when he was mean, he had a smile on his face. When he was on the ice and he had a smile, it was time to look out. I remember a practice session in Gordie Howe's second year — I'd been up about three years — when he decided that we were going to take this old guy into the corner and rough him up. Howe was around nineteen at the time.

Well, Stewart took his left arm and just pinned me across the chest against the screen behind the net so I couldn't even move, and then he lifted Howe off the ice by the shirt in the front of his chest so that his feet were clear off the ice, and just kind of smiled at the both of us. That gives you an idea of his strength.

He hit you clean, with the body, but I do remember once he was mad during a game so he moved his stick about six inches and fractured a guy's wrist, right through the glove. Stewart used to carry a stick with a very thick shaft and blade — stiff as if the shaft was made of steel — and it was at least twice as heavy as the sticks they use today.

One of Stewart's toughest battles was a classic encounter with Johnny Mariucci, the hard-rock Chicago Blackhawk defenseman who had played football for Minnesota's Golden Gophers under coach Bernie Bierman. As the Hawks' policeman he protected the lighter, artistic players like the Bentley brothers and Bill Mosienko.

It was December 4, 1946. In the second period the Red Wings' Syd Howe put Doug Bentley into the boards. Max Bentley didn't like Howe's technique and jumped in to take on Sid Abel as well as Howe.

Referee King Clancy had not seen the Hawks' Alex Kaleta slashed earlier in the game, and in the third period he failed to observe Stewart cutting Mariucci. When Johnny lashed back, Clancy was looking and sent him to the penalty box. At the time, blood was running down Mariucci's face. One writer noted that he must have been penalized for "spilling gore on the ice."

The enraged Mariucci went after Stewart, and they fought on the ice. Sent to the box they continued brawling there, the blood streaking Johnny's uniform, until finally they were ejected from the game. The combat lasted 15 minutes in all, one of the longer fights in NHL history involving only two players.

Toronto's Bills — Barilko and Ezinicki

"Bashing" Bill Barilko had the body of a bronco and the brashness of a gate-crasher. He skated so poorly that he would run several yards on the points of his blades to build up speed. His sense of strategy was crude, but he developed his "snake hips" bodycheck so well that opponents stayed away from his side of the ice as much as possible.

In November 1950 the Rangers were off to a fine start, and one of the reasons was the play of their 155-pound right wing, Jackie McLeod. Then, at Maple Leaf Gardens, Barilko fractured McLeod's collarbone with a check Bobby Hewitson found "uncalled for" in his Toronto *Telegram* report. The former referee wrote that no penalty had been whistled, but that the deliberate crash by the Leaf defenseman was indeed a foul.

Barilko, whose curly blond locks verged on being the NHL's first "Afro" or "Harpo," joined the Leafs from the minor league Hollywood Wolves during the 1946–47 season. In the fifth game of the Stanley Cup finals between the Leafs and Canadiens on April 21, 1951, he scored at 2:53 of the first overtime to give Toronto the Cup. It was his last game. In August a single-engine plane in which he was flying crashed in the forests of northern Ontario, and was lost forever.

If there was one Leaf around whom controversy swirled, fights evolved, and injuries — to the other team — emanated, it was "Wild Bill" Ezinicki. He was not a large man (5'10", 170 pounds), but his biceps and other assorted muscles in his torso were always rippling from regular weight-lifting exercises. He particularly enjoyed free skating and, perhaps even more so, hitting. "I love to bodycheck," said Ezinicki. "I don't care if they bodycheck me. In fact, I love that, too."

Another passion was for tape. He wound rolls and rolls of it around his stick, knees, and shoulder guards.

In a game against the Bruins he had four teeth knocked out but returned to score the winning goal. He had the same kind of insurance policy as Jack Stewart, $5 for each stitch. "It's like double indemnity," said Ezinicki.

He liked to hit from all angles. Sometimes he met the opposition head-on, bending over at the last moment to send his man flying over his back in a manner also favoured by the Rangers' Bill Moe. His favourite method was the "Ezzie Orbit." Montreal defenseman Glen Harmon explained it.

> He'd circle his own defense and catch an opposing puck
> carrier circling from the far side of the defense. We were
> playing against him once, and Ken Reardon came down in
> a mad rush. He was off balance, circling, head down, the
> knees bent, frantically concentrating on retaining
> possession of the puck when Ezzie caught him with what we
> called "the Ezinicki iron shoulder pad" — a regular
> shoulder pad reinforced with tape.
>   Ezzie's shoulder caught Kenny squarely on the jaw.
> Kenny went down with a crash, rolled over, lurched
> unsteadily on his knees, then to his skates. His legs were so

wobbly he looked like he was giving one of those comic
drunk routines. His eyes were actually crossed.

The Canadiens tried to stop Ezinicki by using all kinds of tactics on him. They thought they could beat the Leafs if they could minimize his aggression. Harmon cross-checked him in the face. This went un-detected by the referee, but when others went after Wild Bill, they were apprehended and their penalties led to two Toronto goals. The Leafs won 3–1.

The following week the Canadiens tried to slow Ezzie down again. He took them all on, bashing Maurice Richard so hard on one occasion that the Rocket went through the gate to the Leafs' bench, unhinging it in the process.

In Detroit he was accused of deliberately injuring Red Wing goalie Harry Lumley.

Herb Ralby wrote in the Boston *Globe*: "Toronto has the leading candidate for the most hated opponent in Ezinicki."

In New York, a woman in a front-row seat jammed a long hatpin in Ezzie's derriere as he bent over near the boards on a face-off.

He was on everyone's hate parade except, of course, Toronto's.

On November 8, 1947, Ezinicki folded and spindled Ranger centre Edgar Laprade with a bodycheck. Laprade received a concussion, and his coach, Frank Boucher, fired off an irate telegram to Clarence Campbell. It read: LAPRADE IN HOSPITAL WITH CONCUSSION FROM CHARGE BY EZINICKI AFTER WHISTLE ON OFFSIDE PLAY. REFEREE GEORGE GRAVEL CLAIMS HE DID NOT SEE OFFENSE. HOW MUCH LONGER IS EZINICKI GOING TO GET AWAY WITH ELBOWING, HIGH STICKING AND DELIBERATE INJURIES TO OPPONENTS? BELIEVE CURB MUST BE PUT ON THIS PLAY IMMEDIATELY.

Conn Smythe did not take this accusation lying down. He called on Campbell to fine Boucher $1,000 for "acting in a manner prejudicial to the league." To back up his argument he offered to screen a film of the disputed play for Boucher and six New York writers. When Boucher declined, Smythe retorted, "They don't want to see a legal bodycheck. It might give their players a bad habit."

Campbell then exonerated Ezinicki. "Reports of the officials," he stated, "show that the check by Ezinicki was perfectly legal and not a charge. The injury to Laprade was not caused by Ezinicki's stick but by Laprade striking the ice as he fell."

More than 25 years later Boucher remained unconvinced. "He hurt a lot of players," says Frank. "He charged. He used to play right wing, and he'd watch the fellow carrying the puck. He'd come from nowhere off his wing, and he used to hurt the player because he wasn't expect-ing it.

"In my opinion it was charging, and he should have been penalized a great deal more often than he was. They used to argue that he was bodychecking. The book very distinctly says that if you take more than two or three steps it's charging. Well, if a fellow comes all the way from his wing and hits a fellow almost the other side of the rink you'd hardly call that bodychecking, would you? Ezinicki was rugged but illegal."

Ex-referee Bill Chadwick feels differently. "Ezzie was *not* a dirty player," claims The Big Whistle. "He got penalties because he was rough."

Chapter 5

A GM GOES BERSERK

For the most part, hockey brawls are limited to the ice — but not always.

Every so often an incident explodes away from the actual play itself. Sometimes these incidents can be exceptionally violent. For example, in the early 1960s defenseman Larry Zeidel seethed over an indignity that he insisted forward Eddie Shack had inflicted upon him in an exhibition game. Both Shack and Zeidel had been tossed out of the match and retired to the stands to watch the end of the game. When Zeidel spotted Shack he exploded, leaped to his feet, and jumped Shack right there in the stands. The pair eventually were separated without any great harm done.

There also have been some notable fights in the penalty box, especially in the pre-1960 era, when opposing players shared a penalty box. In one classic incident, Rocket Richard of the Montreal Canadiens stepped into the Madison Square Garden sin bin with Bob "Killer" Dill, a pugnacious Ranger defenseman. Words were exchanged and suddenly the Rocket floored the Ranger with a stiff right cross. Later in the game the pair were penalized again, whereupon Richard reenacted the first bout and flattened Dill once more.

One of the most extraordinary examples of an off-ice eruption took place at the very same Madison Square Garden, only this time the chief protagonists were even more unusual. One was the little general manager of the Rangers, Emile "The Cat" Francis — now an executive with the Hartford Whalers — and the other, the equally diminutive Garden goal judge Arthur Reichert, who, now in his eighties, still holds down that position at Rangers games. In a lesser but nevertheless significant role in this unusual riot were a couple of outspoken fans, not to mention several members of the Rangers, who had to vault the glass at the end boards in order to enter the fray. The story of this unusual incident follows.

Arthur Reichert, a short, wiry man, crouched forward as the Detroit Red Wings headed toward the New York Rangers' zone. It was just past the nine-minute mark in the third period on Sunday night, November 21, 1965, and the Rangers were leading 2–1 at Madison Square Garden. Reichert, who had been a goal judge for more than 20 years, was at his usual position — just behind the Plexiglas barrier at the west end of the arena directly facing the goal cage.

At the same time Emile "The Cat" Francis, the equally small general manager of the Rangers, was sitting somewhere in the side arena urging his defensemen to thwart the enemy attack.

Parker MacDonald of the Red Wings carried the puck over the red line with Norm Ullman, his centre, speeding along at his side. The two Detroiters burst through the New York defense with Ullman now in control of the puck.

As the Wings milled in front of the cage, Ullman swiped at the puck and sent it spinning toward the goal, where Floyd Smith of Detroit added another poke. The Ranger netminder, Ed Giacomin, thrust out his glove hand and nabbed the puck. A split second later Reichert pushed his right thumb against the button and the red light illuminated above the Plexiglas, signalling a Red Wing goal.

The moment Francis saw the red light he leaped out of his seat, dashed along the aisle, and then rushed down to the goal judge's area. By this time five Rangers were milling on the ice directly in front of Reichert, protesting that the puck had never gone in. Francis bulled his way past the spectators surrounding Reichert. "I was watching that play clearly," Francis shouted, "and that puck never crossed the red line."

Reichert, who also happened to be an accomplished tennis player and certified public accountant, stared Francis in the eye and replied, "I've got two witnesses here to prove I'm right."

"I don't give a damn about any witnesses," screamed Francis. "You're the guy who makes the decision and you just made another rotten one."

Suddenly a burly spectator who was sitting near Reichert yelled at the Ranger manager, "Bug off, Francis, that puck was in."

Francis turned to the fan, whereupon another spectator joined the anti-Francis brigade. "One of them," the 150-pound Francis later remembered, "weighed at least 250 pounds."

A flurry of punches spread among the gaggle of fans who surrounded Francis. "Someone, I don't know who, threw the first punch," said Francis, "and things just went from there."

Three spectators jumped him and four men rolled in the aisle directly in front of the protective glass barrier. One fan ripped Francis's jacket off his back while the second crawled on top of the Rangers' boss tossing lefts and rights.

Vic Hadfield, the big, blond Ranger left wing, was looking directly at Francis as the manager went under. Hadfield dropped his gloves and stick, dug his fingers into a small opening between the glass panels, and lifted his skate blades onto the wooden boards. Straining, he pulled himself over the top of the barrier and fell on top of a spectator's seat on the other side. After recovering his balance, Hadfield leaped on the fans who had smothered Francis. "I saw one guy had Francis by the throat," said Hadfield.

One of the spectators pulled away from Francis and fled down the aisle. Meanwhile, Hadfield was followed over the Plexiglas barrier by Arnie Brown, Mike McMahon, Reg Fleming, and Earl Ingarfield of the Rangers. "By this time," said Francis, "the players were all around me. They caught up with the first fan, and then they bagged the second."

Reichert had sidestepped the brawling by moving to an adjacent aisle while the fuss brewed. Garden police moved in to restore order and nobody, not Francis nor any of the fans, pressed charges. "I don't want to press charges," said Francis. "I just want that goal back."

The Rangers did manage to score a goal, but Detroit tied the game less than two minutes from the finish and the contest ended in a 3–3 tie, which served to intensify the bitterness already surrounding the tumultuous scene. Francis and Rangers president William Jennings stormed into the press room and blasted Reichert.

"I had a perfect view of the shot and the puck did not get past Giacomin," Francis insisted. "The light didn't go on immediately, and no one seemed to know who had scored — if you could call it a score. Why, none of the Red Wings even lifted their sticks to signal a goal."

Livid over the fact that referee Art Skov had upheld Reichert's decision, Jennings went a step further and said he would attempt to ban the goal judge from handling Ranger games. "I'm backing up Francis completely," said Jennings. "I am not speaking in haste when I say that Reichert is no longer welcome in Madison Square Garden and there are ways of keeping him out. There are just too many antediluvian minor officials in this league and the Rangers have to do something about it."

Jennings, a National Hockey League governor and one of the most important men in the big-league hierarchy, made his most forceful statement after the game. "The goal judges are employed by the league," Jennings went on, "but he [Reichert] won't get into this building again. Clarence Campbell, the league president, will have to come down from Montreal to get him in."

Needless to say, Ranger goalie Ed Giacomin supported his employer. And naturally Detroit Red Wing coach Sid Abel claimed the puck had gone in. "Certainly," said Abel. "The red light was on, wasn't it?"

"Reichert could have gotten 18 witnesses by going over to the Red Wings' bench," said Francis.

A few days later, tempers had cooled. NHL president Clarence Campbell supported Reichert and insisted that he would continue judging at Garden games. Overruled by Campbell, Jennings had no choice but to permit Reichert in the building. Francis also complied,

and soon all that was remembered was the sight of ten Rangers assault-
ing the glass barrier.

"It was," concluded Francis in a capsule summation of the scene, "a
case of organized confusion."

II

THE ROUGHEST
TEAMS

Chapter 6

THE BIG BAD BRUINS: THE FIRST CHAMPIONSHIP GOON SQUAD

If there was one team which could be accused of introducing the goon era to hockey it was the Boston Bruins under coach Harry Sinden, starting in the 1967–68 season.

At first Sinden appeared to be the Charlie McCarthy to his predecessor Milt Schmidt's Edgar Bergen. But after his rookie season Sinden's own definitive personality took hold, and he began obtaining results. Most of all, Sinden translated Schmidt's hard-hockey policy into reality. "They have changed from a small, meek team that often appeared to be merely going through the motions," wrote Pete Axthelm in *Sports Illustrated*, "into a brawling, powerful unit good enough to lead the league."

They didn't lead the league in points, but they did in boisterousness. They were afraid of nobody and were downright nasty to some clubs. The Rangers were a particular target for abuse, partly because of the smallness of the New York team and partly because of grudges a couple of Bruins nurtured against Ranger players. Once, in a game at Boston, Ted Green knocked Larry Jeffrey of the Rangers unconscious and stood over his foe unchallenged by any New Yorker. Another time Derek Sanderson, then a Bruin rookie, had a fist fight with Orland Kurtenbach of the Rangers, once regarded as the best boxer in hockey, and held Kurtenbach to a draw. It proved, at least, that Sanderson wasn't afraid of *anybody*.

Ruffians seemed to emerge spontaneously in Bruin uniforms previously filled by more placid types. The unity of big men apparently brought strength and hostility. A prime example of the transformation was defenseman Don Awrey. Prior to being teamed with Ted Green, Awrey had been a mediocre defenseman not especially known for his belligerence. By 1967–68 he had rapidly earned a reputation as a brawler, although some opponents suggested he wouldn't be so energetic if Green wasn't at his side on the ice.

"I always had been what you might call a borderline player," said

Awrey. "Never got to play as a regular when I came up in this league. I guess I got to thinking maybe I wasn't aggressive enough. Nobody really advised me . . . although I did talk things over with Teddy Green. I'll tell you something: Just knowing I have him to back me up helps a lot. . . . All I can tell you is that things have changed on this club. In years past if somebody got into a scrap, one or two might join in. Now, on this club, anybody's fight is everybody's fight. That's the way it is."

Wherever the Bruins skated, but especially at home, a rumble was almost certain to develop. In 1967 they assaulted the Canadiens during Montreal's first two trips to Boston, inspiring demands from Montreal coach Toe Blake and general manager Sam Pollock for an investigation to determine, as Toronto *Daily Star* sports editor Milt Dunnell put it, "what kind of ugly pills the Bruins were eating."

When Toronto's general manager–coach Punch Imlach was asked to explain Boston's climb to respectable regions of the NHL, he wasted no time responding, "Because they kick the daylights out of you."

Boston *Globe* writer Chris Lydon detected a cult of toughness on the team after visiting a practice. He recalled seeing Green and Gary Doak waiting near the sideboards for their turn to shoot. "Green backs Doak up against the glass barrier," reported Lydon, "and begins crashing his stick down on the top edge of the glass, inches from Doak's head. 'Let's see how close I can come to your head without you flinchin', eh Doakie?' "

Gerald Eskanazi of the *New York Times* expressed an interesting opinion as the Bruins' influence made itself felt around the NHL. "They seem to be getting paranoid," said Eskanazi. "They think they're always going to be hit by somebody; so they hit first."

The new Bruins psyche had a positive effect on gate receipts in out-of-town rinks, as well as on national publications. People stopped laughing at the Bruins. Opponents viewed them with a mixture of wariness and alarm. They were, in more ways than one, a smash hit.

The Bruins were concerned about winning a high playoff position and managed to land in third place, their highest finish in nine years. They then were routed by the Canadiens in four consecutive playoff games.

"We were congratulating ourselves for finishing third," said Orr, "and before we knew it we were on our way home." Coach Sinden realized more work was needed to mould a genuine challenger for first place and the Stanley Cup.

The 1968–69 Bruins differed only slightly from the previous year's edition, like a late-model car altered only by a few pieces of chrome, some added horsepower, and bigger bumper guards. However, the changes were enough to make Boston a better team than New York and, at times, a better team than the world champion Canadiens. Hard as it may be to believe, the 1968–69 Bruins appeared to be a more belligerent outfit than ever before, as 11 other teams were ready to testify.

By the fall of 1968 word had filtered up and down the hockey grapevine that it was unhealthy to tangle with the Bruins. They had more big, antagonistic men than any other team in the league and they appeared to have no working knowledge of the Marquis of Queensberry rules, nor did they care.

Their basic application of hockey strategy was something like the invasion of Normandy in 1944. First they'd bomb the enemy defenses with heavyweights like Green, Awrey, and Orr; add tough middleweights like Sanderson, Hodge, and McKenzie; then allow all hands to move in and score. That the formula worked is attested to by the record-breaking scoring year enjoyed by Esposito, Hodge, and Orr, to name but a few.

Some foes weren't happy about the fact, but the Bruins undeniably intimidated a select portion of their enemy. Early in the season Mark Mulvoy of *Sports Illustrated* took note of the trend and observed, "The big, bad Bruins gave the Rangers a big, bad beating, both on and off the ice and on the scoreboard." On a trip west after they had pulverized the New York team, the Bruins laughed out loud among themselves about how "the Rangers didn't want any part of the puck."

Obviously, it wasn't just the Rangers. "When they drop the puck to start the game," said Bud Poile, the former general manager of the Philadelphia Flyers, "the Bruins think it is a piece of raw meat. Do they go after it!"

Sports Illustrated observed: "The Bruins also have the league's most vociferous fans. They do not tolerate timid players. The fans particularly dislike players who wear helmets — the Bruins have none." Overlooked, however, were the two Boston goalies, Gerry Cheevers and Ed Johnston, who wore face masks. Did that make them more timid than Montreal's Gump Worsley and Rogie Vachon, who played without such protective gear?

The Boston players seemed to savour their Gashouse role. One of them tacked a Peanuts comic strip on the dressing room bulletin board. It depicted Snoopy, the dog, holding his breath as the final bars of the national anthem were being played. "Ten more seconds," he muttered to himself, "and I can clobber somebody." Somebody pencilled in the word "Greenie." Not long afterward, another Bruin added the caption, "Snoopy could play for us." Another time, forward Glen Sather (now general manager of the Edmonton Oilers) of the Bruins spelled out the motto THINK KILL on the locker-room mirror.

While all this was going on, the team from the Hub climbed right into first place. The Esposito-Hodge-Murphy line became the most overpowering in the league, the defense was rated by *Sports Illustrated* as the best in hockey, and the Bruins seemed hell-bent for their first championship since prewar days.

When the home stretch came into view, Peter Gzowski's interpretation of the Bruins came to mind. "They have, in fact, taken on many of the characteristics of what pool hustlers call 'losers.' Losers lose even when they win a few. They pick up some of the small change but when the big money comes out they go down."

The big money in 1968–69 was first place and the Stanley Cup. Their challengers were the Montreal Canadiens, supposedly weakened by an unknown rookie coach, injuries to starting goalies Gump Worsley and Rogie Vachon in midseason, and the aging of their distinguished captain, Jean Beliveau. There's no way, the experts insisted, that the Bruins can be caught.

Even as a first-place team the Bruins began betraying the characteristics of the losers. Esposito was suspended for two games late in February 1969, when the Bruins could afford it least — for the foolish offence of shoving and hitting a referee. While he was sidelined the Rangers humiliated Boston, 9–0, at Madison Square Garden, to give the Bruins pause.

Injuries, which are more likely to occur on hitting teams, began crippling the Bruins. Tom Williams and Gary Doak were lost for the season. John McKenzie, Bobby Orr, Derek Sanderson, Don Awrey, Ed Johnston, one by one were sidelined for various ailments.

The Bruins' farm system, which had become one of the most productive in the NHL, continued to feed reserves to the big team, and each player looked better than the last. Not surprisingly, they were tough. One of them, Jim Harrison, tangled with tough Gordie Howe, knocked the Red Wing ace's stick to the ice, and then kicked it 30 feet away from him. Schmidt remarked about the lad, "He's what you'd call a disturber."

Studying the close race, coach Sinden predicted that first place in the East Division wouldn't be decided until the final weekend of the season, when Boston and Montreal would meet in a home-and-home series opening in Montreal.

The patrons at Boston Garden could almost taste the championship. They adorned the ancient arena with banners reflecting what Toronto *Globe and Mail* columnist Dick Beddoes described as "Boston's virulent hockey psychosis."

"Play dirty and win!" proclaimed one such adornment. "Sock it to 'em Pie!" said another, in reference to "Pieface" McKenzie. "Tiny Tim doesn't like us — We hate him," announced still another.

All the banners in the world, however, couldn't stimulate the Bruins enough. They were beaten by the Canadiens on the final Saturday night of the season and once more wound up as bridesmaids of the ice.

Conceivably, the loss of first place left Boston fans and the Bruins in an ugly mood on the eve of the first round of the playoffs. They were to meet the Toronto Maple Leafs, the fourth-place team, which had engaged the Bruins in some lively brawls only a few weeks before. In one of them, Pat Quinn, a rather large but clumsy Toronto defenseman, fought with Orr and later told Toronto newsmen that the Bruins' ethics were far to the left of the rule book.

Bruins fans were disturbed about the Quinn incident, especially because Orr was allegedly kicked by the Leaf defenseman. They had hoped he'd appear at the Garden once more during the season, but were disappointed when an injury sidelined Quinn for the Leafs' last regularly scheduled game in Boston.

But when the Leafs and Bruins were paired in the playoffs Quinn was back in action for the opening game and, as one might have anticipated, all hell broke loose. The major fuse was planted in the second period by Quinn and detonated by the Boston fans. For a time it appeared those in the stands would duplicate, or even exceed, their performance against coach Hap Day and defensemen Wally Stanowski and Garth Boesch of the Maple Leafs more than two decades earlier when Boston fans attempted to annihilate the Leafs during a playoff game.

It happened at 18:03 of the middle period, seconds after Orr had picked up speed for a rush along the right boards. "Bobby had his head down," coach Sinden admitted after the contest, "and when you have your head down you have to take your lumps."

Quinn, who had been playing defense in a very one-sided game in the Bruins' favour, detected Orr on his radar. The Leaf rookie rushed Orr from almost a right angle and deposited him on the ice with a devastating check. It remains questionable whether there was anything illegal about the check. Even subjective viewers such as Sinden allow that, at the very worst, Quinn was guilty of charging. "But," said the Bruin coach, "it wasn't a vicious check."

"Quinn hit him with his shoulder," said George Gross, then assistant sports editor of the Toronto *Telegram*.

Orr fell backward on his right hip after the blow and then lay motionless on the ice, face down. Trainer Dan Canney rushed to the scene and, almost immediately, summoned Dr. Ronald Adams, the team physician. At this point referee John Ashley announced that Quinn would receive a five-minute major penalty, instead of the traditional two-minute minor, for elbowing.

"It was quite clear," Gross pointed out, "that Quinn hadn't used an elbow. At worst he should have been given a minor for charging."

In terms of its influence on the game, the penalty was totally irrelevant. Boston held a commanding 6–0 lead and was coasting to victory. Perhaps the award of a major rather than a minor penalty may have suggested to the enraged crowd of 14,659 that Quinn was guilty of hyper-ruthlessness. On the other hand it's conceivable that a few bloodthirsty Boston fans merely wanted a pound of Quinn's flesh and would have started an uprising no matter what the penalty.

Seconds after the Leaf player took his seat in the penalty box some fans crowded around him. The police were conspicuous by their lack of protection for the visiting player. One fan clouted Quinn on the head with his fist while another bounced a hard object off Quinn's skull.

"Boston Garden," Gross observed, "turned into a lunatic bin. The only thing missing was the straitjackets."

An intelligent young man, Quinn realized that his life was in grave and imminent peril, and he sought to protect himself as much as possible. The crowd wasn't satisfied and began a crescendo-like chant that reached deafening proportions. "Get Quinn! Get Quinn!! GET QUINN!!!" — who eventually was forced to seek sanctuary in the Toronto dressing room.

Orr was taken to Massachusetts General Hospital for overnight observation with a slight concussion and a slight whiplash in the neck. X-rays taken at the hospital proved negative, a factor that was unknown to the audience, which remained disturbed as the third period progressed.

They wanted more Leaf scalps and got them late in the period when another brawl erupted, involving Forbes Kennedy of Toronto and several other players.

"Fans leaned over the glass to pound Kennedy," reported Red Burnett in the Toronto *Daily Star*, "while Bruins goalie Ed Johnston had him in a bear hug. . . . There were times when it appeared as if some of the kookier members of the roaring crowd would invade the ice after the Leafs."

All three Toronto papers agreed that the scene was shameful. The Boston *Globe* on April 4 not only carried a lead editorial about the fooferaw but also ran an editorial cartoon depicting Bruin and Leaf players fighting on the ice while a fan tosses beer at Quinn in the penalty box. A plain-clothes investigator stands aside and remarks, "Excuse me, gentlemen . . . I'm from the commission to study violence in America."

At least one Boston writer noted that the Bruins had intimidated the Leafs and there was little evidence to contradict the theory. Boston players laughed among themselves about the "timidity" of some of the visiting players. One of the stories making the rounds had it that a Bruin was mauling a Toronto forward in front of the Boston net. The Bruin expected to be counterattacked.

"Instead," the Boston player related in amazement, "the guy says to me, 'What are you doing that for? I've never done anything to you.' Imagine that!"

NHL official Scotty Morrison added, "This was the dirtiest game I've seen in my four seasons as referee-in-chief and three seasons as an official. It was disgraceful." Yes, it was, but a pattern had been set by the Big Bad Bruins. By 1970 their tough tactics had won them a Stanley Cup and soon their act would be copied by others around the league.

Chapter 7

PHILADELPHIA'S MEAN MACHINE

We take the shortest route to the puck and arrive in ill humour.

The seventh and final game of the 1974 Stanley Cup semifinal playoff between the New York Rangers and Philadelphia Flyers had barely begun when the team from the City of Brotherly Love proved why they were called The Mean Machine, and not The Brotherly Lovers.

One by one — Bobby Clarke, Jim Watson, Rick MacLeish — the Flyers hurled their bodies at the timid Rangers. When the game was nine minutes old, the meanest member of The Mean Machine finally launched himself into battle.

Dave "The Hammer" Schultz, the six-foot-one, 185-pound Flyer left wing, charged at Dale Rolfe, a six-foot-four, 205-pound Ranger defenseman, who was one of the biggest men in the game. It was no contest. Using Rolfe's head as a punching bag, Schultz pounded the helpless hulk of a Ranger into submission while New York players looked on with horror and fear.

"That one-sided victory," said Flyers' coach Fred Shero, "was the turning point of the game. Rolfe's beating took something out of New York. They didn't seem to do as much hitting after that."

No, they didn't. And as a result the Flyers defeated the Rangers 4–3, to win the series and advance to the Stanley Cup finals, where Schultz and Company continued their crusade to raise mayhem to an art form.

Unimpressed by the Boston sextet and their reputation as the Big Bad Bruins, the Flyers came out swinging, taking on the biggest and best of the Beantown swingers. Boston strategists assumed that if Schultz could somehow be destroyed, the Flyers would be routed. So one of the toughest Bruins of all, Wayne Cashman, took on Schultz.

It was a close bout for a while, until Schultz pulled Cashman's yellow-and-white jersey over the Bruin's head and pummelled him with a flurry of lefts and rights. When it was over, the Bruins distributed sour grapes.

Cashman called Schultz "a disgrace to the game" and Bobby Schmautz of the Bruins said the Flyers' enforcer was a "clown." Even Mike Hughes, United Press International executive sports editor, got into the baiting act with barbs at Schultz.

"He (Schultz) does not serve the cause of his team by engaging in fisticuffs," lectured Hughes. "Were he a Russian, he probably would have been banished to Siberia long before the Flyers reached the state of becoming the first expansion club with a chance of winning the coveted Stanley Cup."

But in fact, Schultz *did* serve the cause of his team. Only three days after the bout with Cashman, Dave played a pivotal role in the Flyers' 1–0 defeat of the Bruins, providing Philadelphia with its first Stanley Cup, emblematic of hockey's world championship.

The Flyers had finished first in the West Division by thrusting hips, elbows, and fists at their opponents with exceedingly positive results. At the end of the regular season they had 50 victories and 12 ties in 78 games, as well as one of the biggest team penalty totals — 1,750 minutes in all.

The statistics: During the regular season Philadelphia players accumulated 57 fighting penalties, including 20 by Schultz; 25 misconduct penalties, including five by Schultz. In the 16-team league, the Flyers accounted for more than 10 percent of the fighting penalties and 25 percent of the misconducts.

How, then, did the team win hockey games?

"They intimidate the opposition," said the Pittsburgh Penguins' manager Jack Button, "and don't let the opposition intimidate any of their teammates."

Former Montreal Canadiens' coach Scotty Bowman analyzed the Flyers' strategy another way: "The Philadelphia fighters always went after the best players on the opposition and when a Schultz could take on a Bobby Orr or a Phil Esposito, then it's a real advantage for the Flyers."

But the Flyers' extraordinary success was not rooted in violence alone. They won because they orchestrated ability with hostility. Their goaltender, Bernie Parent, was the best in professional hockey and in 1974 won the Conn Smythe Trophy as the most valuable performer in the playoffs. Centre Rick MacLeish was the leading scorer in the Stanley Cup round and captain Bobby Clarke was generally acknowledged to be the most tenacious checker throughout the season.

"You don't have to be a genius to figure out what we do on the ice," Clarke explained. "We take the shortest route to the puck and arrive in ill humour."

Readily acknowledging their truculence, the Flyers made a distinction between robust and dirty play. Philadelphia skaters insisted that they were not dirty, and even some of their opponents supported their case.

"You've got to respect Schultz," said Montreal Canadiens' defenseman Pierre Bouchard. "When Schultz comes at you, he drops his gloves and stick. He never uses the stick."

Schultz frequently said that he didn't enjoy hurting people in a fight. "I like to beat them up and leave them with some bruises," he asserted, "but I don't want to hurt them. One night I cut Bryan Hextall during a fight in Atlanta and when I saw the blood, I told him I hadn't intended to cut him. And I meant it."

What worried NHL leaders was Philadelphia's astonishing popularity as a fighting team. Some observers believe the Flyers' Mean Machine started a gory trend that spilled unprecedented amounts of blood over the NHL in seasons that followed.

"This year," said one NHL official, a season after Philadelphia won the Cup, "there will be six or eight clubs fighting as much as the Flyers fought last year when they won the Cup."

Few critics of the Flyers ever bothered to examine the roots of their rioting. Actually, it all started as a result of the Philadelphia skaters being pushed around by brutes on the Bruins and St. Louis Blues.

Flyers' president Ed Snider finally had had enough, and ordered his manager, Keith Allen, to stock the club with rugged skaters. Allen followed through on the command. The Flyers became the most popular — and heavily criticized — team in hockey.

"We're getting maligned pretty badly now," said Allen in 1974. "Sure, we're involved in a lot of fights. Sure, we play a physical game. In the Cup finals Boston challenged us just as much as we challenged them, yet we're the bad guys.

"My mother, my own mother, called from western Canada to tell me how bad the Flyers are. Listen, I can remember when I was coaching the Flyers and was embarrassed to take them into Boston and St. Louis. The players knew they would get the hell kicked out of them. Half of them didn't want to even go on the ice. So now we're fighting fire with fire."

That the Flyers' philosophy worked was evident by their success quotient. By employing the same belligerent tactics in 1974, they were able to win a second straight Stanley Cup a year later. Schultz and his henchmen remained at the top of the league in 1975–76, bulldozing their way to the Stanley Cup finals against the Montreal Canadiens.

The 1976 battle for the Stanley Cup was regarded by the media as a test of good versus evil. The Montrealers, headed by the lyrical Guy Lafleur, represented the artistic side of hockey, and many thoughtful Canadien players openly loathed the Flyers and everything they stood for.

"People have asked me which was my favourite Stanley Cup," says

Hall of Famer goalie Ken Dryden, who was in the Montreal nets in the spring of 1976. "Many people think it was my first one in 1971 when I was a rookie. But that's not true. It was in 1976. I hated the Flyers and that was the only team I ever hated."

Dryden's defenseman, Larry Robinson, defused the Flyers by neutralizing Schultz. The Canadiens won the finals in four straight games, ending the Flyers' two-year Cup reign.

The Flyers' high command soon perceived that Schultz's powers of intimidation were leaving him, as the Hammer lost several fights. Finally, in a shocking move, general manager Keith Allen traded Schultz to the Los Angeles Kings at the end of the 1975–76 season.

Interestingly, Schultz was replaced by Paul Holmgren, who, on the Kings' first visit to the Spectrum, wasted Schultz in a fight. The Philadelphians maintained their truculence through the end of the 1970s and into the new decade with considerable success. In 1979–80, they finished with a league-leading 116 points (48–12–20) and reached the Stanley Cup finals, but they were beaten four games to two by the New York Islanders.

By this time, the Flyers had become synonymous with mean hockey, and management consistently replenished the stock of sock men in an attempt to maintain the image of the mid-1970s champions. A parade of ruffians moved through the Spectrum doors. Some of them, like Dave Hoyda — a very poor imitation of Schultz — lasted only two years. Others, like Holmgren, became permanent members of the tough group.

When Holmgren began slipping, other heavyweights moved in. The closest thing to a Hammer Schultz was six-foot-five, 205-pound Dave Brown, who made his debut in the 1982–83 season. Like Schultz, Brown had modest hockey skills but was a terror with his fists. And he occasionally used his stick on an enemy if he believed it was warranted. One night Brown became alarmed at the sight of Ranger forward Tomas Sandstrom jamming the Philadelphia goalie. Brown charged Sandstrom, cross-checking him in the head from behind. Although Sandstrom was not badly injured, Brown was censured across the continent for his behaviour.

In time Brown — much in the manner of Schultz — was deemed expendable and other sluggers were signed. It hardly was surprising that Philadelphia wound up with one of the meanest-spirited goaltenders in hockey history, Ron Hextall. However, the effectiveness of the Flyers' Mean Machine diminished by the end of the 1980s. In 1989–90 and 1990–91, the Broad Street Gang missed the playoffs. And, for the first time in nearly two decades, Philadelphia hockey fans began wondering whether the era of goonery had run its course.

III

INDIVIDUAL ENFORCERS OF THE PAST

Chapter 8

TED LINDSAY: TERRIBLE
TED OF THE RED WINGS

Among left wings, Ted Lindsay was, pound for pound, as competent and mean as any NHL player in the 75 years of big-league play.

Relatively small in stature, Lindsay achieved fame on the Detroit Red Wings' Production Line with Gordie Howe on right wing and Sid Abel at centre.

Lindsay's toughness was manifested with both fists and stick. He would do virtually anything to beat an opponent, and later in his career expressed his toughness in another way, by daring to form an NHL Players Association in defiance of league owners.

Ted Lindsay was born in Renfrew, Ontario, where his father, Bert Lindsay, played goal for the Creamery Kings of the National Hockey Association, a forerunner of the NHL. As a youngster, Lindsay played hockey on the streets in the winter. "They were always covered with snow," he explained, "because they didn't use sand or salt in those days. My dad had kept his goalie pads and we used them until they fell apart. They really didn't give much protection."

As he grew up, Ted had the chance to play hockey at school because, as he told it, "Every school had two outdoor, natural-ice rinks. One was for skating and one was for hockey. We used to skate on that packed snow from our house to the school early Saturday mornings. We'd go home for lunch, then come back again. It was too cold for anyone to stand around so whoever came to play hockey played all the time. Sometimes we'd have 20 guys out there at once. This is where we learned to stickhandle, and this is where we got conditioning. You simply had to have it. If our school won a championship, our reward was that we got to play in an indoor rink."

It was this kind of background, similar to that of most major leaguers of his era, that readied Lindsay for NHL play. "When I got there," he said, "I discovered that I had to be tough because the other players tested me very quickly. Some of the guys really were tough, but some of them weren't and they'd just try to bluff you. If they were successful, they could run you right out of the rink. I decided that nobody was going to do that to me.

"I was tested by just about everybody when I came into the league. At that time (1944–45), Detroit was rebuilding. It was at the tail end of the war, and there were a lot of fringe players. At that time, I was stupid enough to think that I could beat up everybody in the league — and I tried to do it.

"As it turned out, I won some and lost some. The interesting thing was that I didn't have as much to lose as the big guy I was fighting because everyone expected him to beat me up. But if I managed to win, it was really embarrassing for him."

When he finished the 1,068th game of his career, which spanned 17 seasons before coming to a close after 1964–65, he was the all-time NHL penalty leader with 1,808 minutes. He averaged 106 penalty minutes per season, at a time when they played only 70 games.

In addition to all those penalty minutes, Lindsay amassed 379 goals and 472 assists in regular-season play. You might say he did it all, including bringing along a supply of intangibles that didn't show up in the box scores but won games and earned him a spot in the Hall of Fame.

If there was no argument about his hockey skills, his tactics remained a subject of controversy. Lynn Patrick, general manager of the Boston Bruins in the 1950s, said, "Lindsay is a sneak. He's mean and nasty, and he'll hit you from behind."

Rangers' general manager Muzz Patrick commented, "Pound for pound, there is no one tougher or more vicious than Lindsay."

Maurice Richard was not one of his greatest admirers. "For me," said the Rocket, "the worst player by far whom I've ever skated against was Ted Lindsay. It wasn't so much that he was a dirty player, but as far as I'm concerned, he had a dirty mouth. He swore at everybody on the ice."

One night Richard fought the entire line of Lindsay, Abel, and Howe. He got the best of Lindsay, but the fight tired him. Then Abel hit him. "As I staggered away," he remembers with displeasure, "Howe came along and got the best of me. But it was Lindsay who was the culprit. For sheer troublemaking he was at the top of my list. He was a bad man with everything — his mouth, his stick — and off the ice, believe it or not, it was the same thing. Even his wife would yell and swear at me if she spotted me outside the dressing room at the Olympia Stadium. I'd hear everything in the book from both of them."

Howe remembers Lindsay's verbal darts during play stoppages. "You know conversation plays a very important part out there on the ice," explained Gordie. "Sometimes when the conversation gets crude and one player is after another, we bring these things on ourselves.

"I remember, for instance, when I played with Lindsay, I'd be in the face-off opposite a guy and Lindsay would yell to me loudly, 'Ram the stick through the so-and-so!'

"First thing I know, the puck gets dropped and I get drilled, because the other guy is worried about getting hit himself. Lindsay used to get me in trouble like that a lot."

"Once I'm on the ice I hate everybody wearing a different colour jersey," was Lindsay's philosophy. "I've been slashed, speared, elbowed, butt-ended, and board-checked as much as anybody," he said during his playing days. "I've had a broken shoulder, a broken instep, a broken hand, and about 250 stitches in my face. I just like to keep the ledger balanced. I don't think of hockey players as being unnecessarily dirty — they're just very competitive. When you play against dirty players, they're not really a concern to you because you know who they are and you know how you have to defend against them."

Lindsay was short but strong, and he also utilized other means besides his muscles. "The stick was a great equalizer for me," he frankly admitted. "When you're five foot nine, all of a sudden you become six foot three. I didn't use it much as a weapon — it was more to keep the other fellow honest. I've been in a lot of stick-swinging duels — both as instigator and defender. It's not a good thing, but when the adrenalin gets going you become sort of a Jekyll-Hyde personality. It's like we're in a jungle and it's survival of the fittest. And no one was going to intimidate me."

Ted feels that his competitive spirit was his greatest asset. "I've always hated to lose at anything," he stated, expressing his concern that junior sports programs are creating a "generation of losers." He said that the practice of having kids shake hands with the guy that beats them "gives them the idea that they should be happy about losing."

The way Lindsay played the game there were enough incidents to make the dossier bulge. One night in 1948 the Canadiens were leading the Red Wings by a goal late in the game. Large, swarthy Roger Leger of the Canadien defense found himself with the puck after the face-off, whereupon Lindsay hit him with a jolting bodycheck. His elbow rammed into Leger's bridgework, sending Roger racing to his bench gasping for air. While the false teeth were being extricated from his throat, Detroit tied the score.

Sometimes the ones that miss can be as indelibly etched in your memory as the ones that connect. Long-time Ranger fans still remember the swing that nearly deposited Hy Buller's head in the side arena.

Lindsay was given a ten-day suspension for striking a spectator with his stick in a game at Toronto on January 22, 1955. It started with a scuffle between Eric Nesterenko and Gordie Howe along the boards. A

Leaf fan grabbed Howe's stick and, as Gordie pulled away, reached over the boards in an attempt to hit him. Lindsay, who was 30 to 40 feet from the action, rushed forward and belted the fan.

I saw him doused by a cup of beer thrown over the glass at a corner of the Garden in New York. Lindsay, then with the Chicago Blackhawks, clambered atop the boards and held the edge of the glass with one hand. What he couldn't reach with his stick, he could with his mouth, so he spit at the fan and followed with some choice invective. Finally, he had to be hauled down from his perch so the game could continue. The fan was lucky.

In February 1957, Lindsay put Boston's Jerry Toppazzini in the hospital for a month. "It was in Detroit and we were behind by a goal," recalled Lindsay. "We pulled our goaltender before a face-off in their end. I was coming in and the puck was shot from the blueline. One of the Boston defensemen stopped it and I got possession. I kind of had my head down on my feet as I got the puck and as I passed it, I saw this Bruin. I saw him coming towards me, and it's an instinctive move for self-protection that if a fellow was going to get at me I brought my stick in a cross-check position. I figured if a guy's going to get at me he's got to go through my arms, and when he gets to my body it might hurt but it's not going to hurt as much. So I brought my stick up and I don't know if Jerry was a little bit lower than normal or if I brought my stick up, but I cross-checked him right across the face. He went down like somebody had hit him with a car. I could tell he was hurt seriously when he was down on the ice because of the blood being very thick."

The next day a concerned Lindsay went to the hospital to visit Topper. "I felt badly," he said, "even though he was an enemy, an opponent. We hate to lose, but we don't want to maim."

What he saw was a face fractured in numerous places. "I couldn't believe how badly disfigured it was," he said later. "It didn't even look human. It was swollen just to a round ball. I got a sick feeling in my stomach."

After the 1959–60 season, Lindsay left the Blackhawks and went into retirement. He returned in 1964–65 for one more season with the Red Wings before hanging up his skates permanently.

Chapter 9

THE ZANY PLAGER BROTHERS OF ST. LOUIS

It isn't often that a boisterous brother act teams up on one club and is able to last for a relatively long period of time, but the exception was Bob and Barclay Plager of the St. Louis Blues.

The siblings from northern Ontario not only helped drive St. Louis to the Stanley Cup finals in 1968, 1969, and 1970, but they wreaked havoc throughout the league with their rugged tactics and general air of boisterousness.

In addition to their raw talent as defensemen they also could handle their dukes. Bob became notorious for his "snake hips" bodychecks. Barclay was one of the finest shot-blockers in the business. No pair of NHL hit men did their nasty work with more humour.

By the time Barclay and Bob Plager joined the Blues in 1967 for their inaugural season, between them they had kicked around a dozen minor league cities, leaving a trail of laughter and bruised bodies in their wake. It didn't take long to reestablish their credentials as the zaniest guys in hockey — or at least in St. Louis, where they became part-time leaders and full-time court jesters.

Born in 1941 and the oldest of three hockey-playing brothers, Barclay Plager would later become captain of the Blues as he and brother Bob, younger by two years, anchored the club's defense in a style approaching mob violence. Even brother Billy, the youngest, would get into the act for a few seasons. The result was mayhem on the ice and off. "I like to keep the guys loose," said Bob. "I think it's part of my job."

Big Bob's mandate extended all the way up to then Blues' president Sid Salomon III, who once awoke at the end of a team flight to discover that Bob had performed corrective surgery on his tie. Not to be outdone, Sid later snipped off one leg of Bob's pants during a practice.

Bob refused Salomon's offer to pay for the pants, but a week later he showed up at a fashionable party thrown by Sid III in the same abbreviated set of pants. Then, and only then, would he accept a check.

On ice, the Plagers' impact has been described as "gang warfare," a bruising brand of hockey that had its roots in Kirkland Lake, Ontario, where the boys first laced on skates.

"When we were young," said Bob, "Barclay used to beat me up so I used to beat up Bill who'd go across the street and beat up our little cousin, all in the same day. In junior hockey we had one of the greatest fights they ever saw in the league."

The brothers didn't make the jump from Kirkland Lake to St. Louis without a bit of assistance. Their father, Gus, was a promising hockey player himself until his career was cut short by an injury. Gus Plager then became a referee, as well as a coal miner like so many men in the town. You have to go underground to understand why the Plager boys took up skating.

"We had two choices when we were growing up," said Bob. "Go into professional hockey or go into the mines."

All three Plagers began skating together, and scrapping, at an early age. "When we lived in Kirkland Lake, we had a big field behind the house," Gus Plager once recalled. "If the boys got into an argument, they'd go out back and fight. One would get the better of it and that would end it. I thought that was a good way of settling things."

Occasionally, the boys would go too far. One night when they were still playing junior hockey, Barclay — accidentally, he claimed — jammed his stick in Bob's mouth and Bob responded with his fists. "We went at it pretty good on the ice," Bob remembers, "but they broke it up. As we went into the penalty box he gave me a shove and we started fighting again. Then, after we were thrown out of the game, we continued to battle in the runway leading to the dressing rooms. But I got the best of him for the first time.

"Afterwards I met him in a restaurant across the street from the rink. I was sitting there eating when he walked in. We looked at each other and I didn't know what was going to happen. The whole Guelph team rushed into the place to see.

"Everyone figured we'd go at it again, but Barclay just looked me in the eye and said, 'Can you lend me five dollars?' "

Bob, the most injury prone of the Plager brothers, played briefly for the New York Rangers in the midsixties. And one year, shortly before the opening of training camp, he fell off a cliff in Kapuskasing, banging his ankles and various other parts of his anatomy. What was he doing there, management wondered? "Running to get in shape," was Bob's explanation.

The New York front office soon became attuned to Bob's sense of humour. "One day," recalled former Rangers' publicist John Halligan, "he picked up a portable radio I had sitting on my desk. I thought he only wanted it for a few days at his hotel. When he returned the next week I asked where it was. 'Oh,' he said, 'I just mailed it home to my mother.' The next week he picked up the instruction book that came with the radio. I suppose he sent that home, too."

Bob later parlayed a tall tale about his off-season activities into a near court case. He said that he was a beer taster in a Kapuskasing brewery. "I take sample sips to see if the beer is stale or not," he told reporters. Soon the Ontario Brewers' Retail Association received offers from others wanting the same sinecure. The brewers group challenged the story, and threatened to take action. Actually, Bob just drove a beer truck.

Such shenanigans did not exactly endear Robert to the Rangers and soon he was traded to St. Louis. Barclay, also briefly Rangers property, never even played a game for the New Yorkers.

The Blues were willing to give both of them a try. In June 1967 they picked up Bob in a deal for defenseman Rod Seiling, who would return to the Blues for the 1976–77 season, and in November of that year Barclay came to St. Louis along with Red Berenson in a deal for Ron Stewart and Ron Atwell.

A year later, brother Billy, the youngest of the triumvirate, came to the Blues in a trade with the Rangers, and for a few years the three Plager boys were together on the same team.

"They come to play," said Scotty Bowman, then Blues coach. "I don't have to worry about them being up for a game. And they're no trouble to sign. They come in, ask what they're worth, and sign their contracts."

Added General Manager Lynn Patrick, "I've never seen guys like them. All they talk about is hitting. We can use it. They're nice kids, though, and that Bob is a quick one with a comeback."

Once when Bob missed the team plane after a game in New York, he told a furious Patrick that he'd never believe the reason for his absence.

"Try me," said Patrick.

"Well," said Plager. "I woke up in the hotel, looked at the clock, and it was 11:30. The plane had left at 11:00. I looked up at the ceiling, closed my eyes and said, 'Why me? Why does it always have to be me?'

"Lynn, I told you you'd never believe it. The ceiling opened up and a large hand came through, a finger pointing down at me. And then this loud voice said, 'Because I don't like you.' "

One observer reported that Bob "punches like ex-heavyweight champ Sonny Liston but sometimes skates like him, too." Bob's response? "I skate better than Liston."

In 1990–91 Bob coached the International Hockey League's Peoria Rivermen, who set a professional hockey record with 18 consecutive wins early in the season.

Tragically, Barclay succumbed to a brain tumour in February 1988, just days before the NHL All-Star game in St. Louis. The pregame ceremonies honoured Barclay, with family in attendance.

Chapter 10

LARRY ZEIDEL: THE TOUGHEST JEWISH DEFENSEMAN

Over the years the NHL has been graced with outstanding Jewish defensemen, including Alex "Kingfish" Levinsky of the Maple Leafs and Hy Buller of the Rangers. But the toughest Jewish backliner of all was Larry Zeidel, who made his NHL debut in 1951–52 with the Stanley Cup champion Detroit Red Wings and concluded his career in 1967–68 with the Flyers.

Zeidel's turbulent saga makes an interesting case study of a big-league bad guy. As a youth, he was subject to anti-Semitic abuse in his lower-class Montreal neighbourhood. Rather than turn the other cheek, Zeidel fought back and eventually developed the truculent personality that usually stood him in good stead on the ice rink.

Larry worked his way up to the NHL via a circuitous minor league route but never lost sight of his ultimate goal. When he reached the top, he found himself side by side with some of the roughest hombres this side of the O.K. Corral. They included "Terrible" Ted Lindsay, Gordie Howe, and Glen Skov.

Employing a swashbuckling style of defending — Zeidel never thought twice about using his stick as a bayonet, if wartime conditions called for such behaviour — Larry earned a reputation throughout North American hockey rinks.

Some of Zeidel's bouts became the stuff of hockey legends, including a stick fight with Jack "Tex" Evans that is considered the single bloodiest one-on-one duel in the annals of organized hockey. Zeidel survived this and other less gory (but no less intense) battles over the years.

Not surprisingly, Larry was the target of hockey bigots in the NHL as well as the minors. By far his most memorable encounter took place when as an NHL senior citizen he was confronted by members of the Boston Bruins and ultimately wound up in a stick fight — not unlike the Evans encounter — with Eddie Shack.

Although Zeidel was one of the better Flyers defensemen on a first-place team, he was not invited back the following year. To this day there

is some question as to whether his challenge to the hockey establish-
ment via the anti-Semitic charges against the Bruins resulted in his
removal from the scene.

Currently a Philadelphia stockbroker, Zeidel still relishes rough
hockey and makes no apologies for his deportment during his long
reign as a pro.

Larry Zeidel grew up in the tough Park Extension section of Montreal
where his family were the only Jews in the neighbourhood. When he
was six, some kids jumped his ten-year-old brother, and he stood by,
unable to help. Then he felt the sting of anti-Semitism even more
personally. "The kids knew I was a Jew," he said. "They'd gang up on
me. First it was one giant, then another. These kids get implanted in
your mind."

To ensure his survival, Zeidel had to beat up the class bully all the
way up the ladder in public school. This way he built a reputation, and
soon he was left to go about the normal childhood pursuits without
harassment. Later, he translated his tactic to hockey. Without it he
would have been run out of any league in which he tried to compete.
Refusal to be intimidated, as we know, is one of the primary survival
rules in the sport. Being Jewish, in that era, underlined this credo for
Larry.

Zeidel played junior hockey under Hap Emms, who told him, "Get
punchy. You play better when you're punchy," and "Give them shots
when the referee isn't looking." Later, player-coach Punch Imlach
picked up Zeidel, along with a few others, to play for his Quebec Aces.

When Zeidel was with Imlach's Aces, Quebec was a senior amateur
club. In addition to playing in their own Quebec League, they played
home games against the Eastern Amateur Hockey League, which
included the New York Rovers, a Ranger farm team. "The Rovers had a
Chinese player named Larry Kwong who was scoring quite a few
goals," relates Zeidel. "Imlach told us, 'They've got one threat,' and
Imlach wasn't really a hitter. He was small.

"I was just a kid learning about hockey. The game starts and prac-
tically the first play, Kwong is concentrating on beating one defenseman and Imlach cuts across and catches him, blindside, and knocks
him out cold."

As a twenty-three-year-old, Zeidel played in 19 games with Detroit
during the 1951–52 season. The following year he appeared in nine
games with the Wings. His first full season in the NHL was with
Chicago in 1953–54. There he fought the whole Montreal bench because Bert Olmstead grabbed his stick. "You've got to show some life
when you're the underdog, eh," he commented.

Then it was back to the minors again until 1967. In cities like
Edmonton, Hershey, Seattle, and Cleveland he built a reputation as a
wild man — a stick-wielding brawler who was liable to erupt at any

time. When he played for Hershey, they hated his guts so much in Cleveland that a fan threw a chair at him, but when he showed up in a Cleveland Baron uniform they loved him.

One of the early incidents that helped build the Zeidel legend occurred when he punched Phil Maloney into the hospital. Edmonton was playing the Vancouver Canucks in a Western League game, and Maloney was at centre for the Canucks. He had been with Boston and Toronto for a couple of years and, according to Zeidel, was "schooled in the Hap Day, Toronto, clutch-and-grab style. Win 1–0 or 2–1, that was the way Hap Day played it."

On this particular night Maloney took his stick to Zeidel's crotch on a face-off. Larry took offence, and they scuffled, ending up in the penalty box. Then one of the Canucks began chasing an Edmonton player around the ice. "Somebody had to go out there because it was embarrassing to see one of our guys running away from one of their guys," Larry reasoned. "So I left the penalty box and got kicked out of the game."

As he left the ice to take a shower, Zeidel spotted Maloney still in the penalty box, which was right next to the exit to the dressing room. "He had really gotten me in the nuts," emphasizes Zeidel. "When you're young you're emotional. I planted him one — hit him so goddamned hard that the ambulance came and took him to the hospital. His eyes were funny."

Zeidel's notoriety was spread further by a gory stick fight with Saskatoon's Jack Evans, former coach of the Hartford Whalers. After a while, the mention of his name would be accompanied by a knowing look that said, "Look out for the crazy man."

Zeidel cites a brouhaha in the AHL as "one of the few times in my life I got a break." Referees and league presidents had made him a marked man, and he usually got two minutes just for showing up and another two for looking mean.

"I'm playing defense with Howie Young for Hershey against Springfield," he recalled, "and Kent Douglas is coming down. He could skate. Next year he went to Toronto and won the rookie award. He was frustrated because we didn't go for his moves. We didn't give him the hole that he wanted. And in frustration he literally shoved his stick down my throat. He caught me back in the Adam's apple, and the old Adam's apple went right here somewhere and I blacked out momentarily. Howie Young didn't like it, and he started to fight. When I came to, Young was battling with Douglas. I was so goddamned mad. I didn't go into the game high, but when somebody does something like that to you.... I took my stick and whacked him one while he was still fighting with Young. And they were still wrestling around, blood all over both of them. They continued to fight too long and were thrown out of the game. I didn't even get a penalty."

It is amazing how players can deal so viciously with each other on the ice and not carry deep-seated grudges forever. Ed Van Impe and Claude Laforge were not the only feudists to kiss and make up on the brand-new Philadelphia Flyers in 1967–68. Another compatible couple was Zeidel and Pat Hannigan. In fact, Larry *suggested* Pat for the team when, by all reason, you would think he would rather fix him a Raid cocktail.

"Here's an example of how players forgive," Zeidel stated. "I'm playing for Seattle, and I didn't want to play any dirty hockey. I'm thirty-five and I'm playing for Keith Allen. But then there was this big write-up — public relations, promotional — like I'm Jesse James, Billy the Kid, name them all and I'm all of that combined; psycho and the whole goddamned bit from all the headlines with Evans, Shack, Bailey, and Phil Maloney.

"So I'm a dirty, rotten so-and-so but I said, 'The hell with it, I'm not going to do it. There's too much wear and tear. I'm thirty-five. I can play it straight.' And I took more shit in that league trying to prove that I wasn't dirty. Once in a while, I felt guilty because this team we had wasn't too rugged, and Portland used to rough us.

"I wouldn't go in high. I'd sit on the bench and think, 'I'm just going to do my job,' but then they'd get bullied a little so maybe I'd have to hit back but nothing dirty. Jack Bionda would be running around, Con Madigan. Our guys were running scared, eh, into losing. So finally I hit a few guys, nothing dirty, not like in Cleveland. They only had two referees, Gilmour and Papp.

"So now we're playing Portland. Bionda's running from one end of the rink to the other, running at our guys. But I don't blame him. They're running scared. Why not? He wasn't doing it dirty, just really pounding them into the boards. The guys were quitting. But Portland's not getting penalties for it. It's charging.

"So in this game I decide to bump a few guys. 'Two minutes, Zeidel. Charging.' And I wasn't really charging. These guys were really hitting little Guyle Fielder and guys like that. Now I'm not stirred up. You've got to be with a group. It wouldn't do me any good to get fired up on that Seattle team. There were too many guys who would lay down. They weren't moulded like a Boston. You don't want anyone to admire the opposition, and that team was a bunch of losers. Right at training camp they were admiring the opposition and how great it is in Portland — and talking about everything but our one goal, to win.

"Well, now I've got three minors. I better take it easy. Pat Hannigan's coming down the right wing and he's cutting in to centre. And I'm still a competitor. I can't get any more penalties, but I move out to stop him. You know, you don't want to back in. I've got him lined up so he can't get in there. Two hands on the stick.

"I'd been around long enough to know better than to have a stick down there, because if you both bring them up nobody gets hurt. Part of defending yourself. I do my job. I'm defense. You're offense. If you don't want to bring your stick up, outfox me, outdeke me. Fake me out of my jockstrap, take me out for coffee. But if you figure you make a pass and I got ya, we both get 'em up.

"Well I had my stick down and that Hannigan, that goddamned stick sunk into my skull, just sunk in — I've got a scar from here to here — and pushed my hair back like I was scalped. You can ask Keith Allen. It was the worst he ever saw.

"In Detroit you'd have Academy Awards for guys that would lay down when they were hurt. It was all in fun. Tony Leswick would win the award for best actor. It was part of getting the message across of 'Play when you're hurt.' Okay. No way — I don't give a damn if I have torn knee ligaments — I'm going to go to the trainer because I was moulded the way Hitler moulded his goddamned youth. I fought with everybody; hacked them up.

"Now with Hannigan, here I am bleeding like a stuck pig, but I didn't get knocked out and I'm awake and thinking, 'You son of a bitch. You're lucky I don't rap your head, but if I do they throw me out of hockey.' I've got a reputation: 'Well, that Zeidel, he uses his stick. He's dirty. We heard about that fight with Jack Evans. He's a stick man. He's a hatchet man.'

"So I'm thinking. All I did was talk to Hannigan. 'You dirty bastard. You're lucky I don't hit you.' I'm talking, instead of an eye for an eye and a tooth for a tooth.

"Then I go in to get stitched up, and I've been stitched up many a time. I know what it's all about, and these doctors, they take their time. I'm lying there, and I want to get back out there and play because, over the years, if you're a good competitor, any time the opposition injures you and you come back, you've got them psyched. That's why we [Edmonton] won the championship over Saskatoon.

"This doctor gets me in there, and he must figure I'm a dirty son of a bitch from the opposition. He takes towels and puts them all over my face and I can't breathe and I can't hear. It's like he's performing an operation.

"He hasn't even started to stitch me yet but he's smothering me. And I'm moving the towels away. I'm in no state to take any shit. And he loses his patience with me and starts giving me hell. They look at me as if I'm nuts and they're saying, 'Take it easy, take it easy.' "

With the coming of expansion in 1967, Larry "The Rock" Zeidel, thirty-nine-year-old defenseman, sent out a brochure to all the teams, promoting himself as player, coach, or executive. It included an affidavit from a doctor stating that he had the heart of a twenty-year-old. Only a few organizations had the courtesy to answer. One signed him — as a player. It was Philadelphia, where Bud Poile was general manager and Keith Allen the coach — two men for whom Zeidel had played. When Poile asked him for his appraisal of personnel in the American League, Zeidel recommended Hannigan. "So at least I'm honest," Larry said. "I told him to get Hannigan. He'd hit his mother to win that next game. A lot of the so-called experts said the Flyers wouldn't make it, that Philly's a basketball town, a conservative town. But they got guys like Hannigan, Forbes Kennedy and that helped to sell hockey in Philadelphia."

With Zeidel as a key man in the spirit department and a steadying influence on defense, the Flyers finished first, but not without trial and tribulation. Poile said of his thirty-nine-year-old rearguard, "He's too old to be a hatchet man. But he's a winner. He's been a winner all his life."

In his new role Zeidel, a man who had led three different leagues in penalty minutes, twice going over 200 minutes with Hershey, was doing his best to stay out of trouble. It didn't always work.

The Flyers and St. Louis Blues, although brand-new rivals, quickly developed a loathing for each other. In the course of one game, Flyer defenseman Ed Van Impe speared Blue rookie Gordon Kannegiesser. Both benches emptied.

This event occurred at the end of the game, but it was also before the stringency of the "third-man rule" and other legislation concerning leaving the bench. "You'd probably lose your job if you didn't leave the bench," said Zeidel. "But you're damned if you do and damned if you don't. This particular game, I didn't even play. I was cold. The game was over. I went on the ice. I was just standing around. Picard saw me nearby and boom, he sucker-punched me. I didn't like that so I started a fight with him. What do I get for it? I get my name in the paper. I get a letter from Campbell. I get fined for leaving the bench."

Late in the season, toward the end of February, there was trouble at the Spectrum, home rink of the Flyers. A powerful wind tore a hole in the roof of the structure. On March 1 some stronger gusts did even more damage, and the building was closed. The Flyers, battling to win their division, had to take to the road. First they played a "home" game in New York; then, on March 7, 1968, they skated out against the Boston Bruins at Maple Leaf Gardens. If Maple Leaf fans were not prepared for Philadelphia as their "home" team, they were even less ready for the bloody imbroglio that followed. The principals were old antagonists, Zeidel and Eddie Shack, a former Toronto favourite.

The two first met in the late 1950s when Shack was a rookie coming up to the Rangers and Zeidel was with Hershey, training that season at Niagara Falls, Ontario. Crew-cut Eddie was rough and rangy, with a nose that could have served well on the front of an ice-breaker. Zeidel spotted him in an exhibition game and mused, "He'll go good in New York." Soon there was another exhibition game in Niagara Falls. This time it was the Rangers versus Hershey.

Zeidel had been inculcated with the expression they used in Detroit, "Give 'em the lumber." When he laid a little wood on Shack, Eddie cut him. "He had a short fuse," Larry recalled. "I'm bleeding and he hasn't got a scratch on him. My teammates are telling me, 'Take it easy, Larry.' "

After Zeidel was stitched up, he went to the stands to watch the rest of the game. Who does he see on the opposite side of the rink but Shack. "People are crowding around him, getting his autograph," related Larry. "I'm still burning. I get cut open, and this kid's smiling and taking all the pats on the back. So I walked around, tapped him on the shoulder, and I planted him one. Okay? He called it a sucker punch. You know he turned around this way and his knees buckled. So I had the edge. Like they say, get the first one in. Right. So then I was in a state of mind where I really wanted to fix his clock. Then this cop grabbed me from behind. He threw me down and on my back, and then came down on me with his knees in my face."

When Hershey captain Obie O'Brien came to Zeidel's aid, he was arrested, too, and taken to the police station with his equipment still on. The two Hershey players were fingerprinted, Zeidel's belt was removed, and they were thrown in the drunk tank. "We're in separate cells," Zeidel said. "They finally bailed us out at 1:30. Next day the headlines read Zeidel Attacks . . . Every referee or would-be referee read that."

The same day, Zeidel appeared in court. The judge found him guilty and gave him a suspended sentence.

Before going round two with Shack, Zeidel took a lot of flak from Eddie's Bruin teammates — in January, for example, when the Flyers faced the Bruins at Boston Garden in an afternoon TV game. Zeidel had been getting many favourable write-ups about his effective play and, naturally, the fact that he was staying away from the rough stuff drew approving commentary.

Before the game, as the teams were at centre ice, shooting to warm up the goaltenders, Ted Green, the resident bogeyman, skated over to Zeidel and threatened him. "He was high," Zeidel said. "I've gone into games high, like sharpening a stick. I've been there before. So nobody in hockey is going to teach me about 'getting' for intimidating. I've been there. The easiest way to win a game is by intimidation. You have a holiday. You don't even work up a sweat."

In January 1968, the Flyers were leading the West Division. Boston took a 2–0 lead. Philly countered with a goal. Then, with a Bruin already in the penalty box, Green rushed down the ice with the puck. "He's sky high like I used to get," Zeidel explained, "but I'm going in low-key — the dial is not on high. You turn the dial any way you want, low or high.

"He takes a shot on the net and he keeps going. He shoves the stick down my throat, and I get knocked right into the net. I know how to take care of myself. Let him run me into the goddamned net. But I keep cool. We've been successful going that way."

Teddy was not just trying to make his threat good. He was attempting to even a score for his fellow defenseman, Don Awrey. Prior to Green's rush, Awrey had taken a "good run at me," said Zeidel. "I gave him the elbow and the lumber. But I went easy on the kid. I could have really given it to him. Now here's the bad joke. This bad man of the NHL, leading the league in penalties, this paper tiger, went and told his daddy [Ted Green]. It's comical. If he's supposed to be tough, when I spear him he's supposed to shove the stick down my throat and take care of his own dirty work."

Green was penalized for his actions and while Boston had two men in the penalty box, the Flyers tied the score. "It looked like the turn-the-other-cheek strategy was working," Larry recalled. "Then, before it's over, they snuck one in to make it 3–2. I played it cool to help prove a point, which I regret. We went back on a chartered plane and I was hurting, not only because we lost but because I was disappointed in myself."

All of a sudden the Flyers started losing close games, and their eight-point lead began to evaporate. Zeidel was very conscious of his plus–minus figures because of bonuses. He told himself, "There's no way we're going to lose in the last five minutes because of me being caught up the ice."

Before the opening face-off on March 7 at Maple Leaf Gardens, the idea that Zeidel was a Bruin target persisted in a pernicious manner. Poile was informed to this effect and, reportedly, brought it to the attention of referee Bob Sloan. Poile stated, "We know that the Bruins warned Larry they were going to get him. It was more than just the idle baiting you hear in most sports."

Early in the first period a Boston shot headed for the Flyers' goal. Derek Sanderson tried to deflect it into the net, but Zeidel, who was covering him, got a stick on it first. The puck jumped up and caught Sanderson under the eye, knocking him down and cutting his face. It hadn't been intentional, but as Derek went off for stitches, the Bruins' mood turned uglier. Their threats became more personal and followed ethnic lines.

Certain Bruins were doing more than calling Zeidel "Jew boy." Shortly after the nine-minute mark, he exploded along with his old foe Eddie Shack, who remembered their earlier encounter. "I was only a rookie at the time of our first battle," he said. "Zeidel speared me twice and I said, 'Spear me again and I'll hit you right over the head.' He speared me again so I let him have it, right over the head."

Zeidel describes how their second encounter started. "Shack is not satisfied just to hit you. He's colourful. I'd like him on my team. I took a shot from the point and he hit me. I high-sticked him." Then the swinging began in earnest. Zeidel opened up the back of Shack's scalp while Eddie carved his initials on Larry's forehead. They ended up in back of the Flyers' net, where the linesmen finally were able to part them. Sloan ejected both with match misconducts.

The next day the story of the Bruins Jew-baiting came out. Zeidel indicated that Shack had no part in it, but he did single out Green, Awrey, Gerry Cheevers, and Tommy Williams as the ringleaders, although Williams had not in fact been in uniform that night. However, he could have been near the vicinity of the Boston bench.

When the unsavoury affair hit the headlines in Toronto and Boston, Bruin coach Harry Sinden claimed he had heard nothing resembling the remarks reputedly passed. "But I don't doubt someone called him 'Jew boy' or something like that on the ice. He was calling Esposito 'Wop.' That doesn't mean they are bigots. We call Tom Williams a stupid American."

Zeidel countered, "That bit about me being a 'Jew boy' is music to my ears." It was something he had heard before and it didn't make a dent. "Trying to shake you up verbally to break up your concentration is all part of the game," he conceded, "but when they start saying things like 'We'll carry you out on a slab and send you to the gas chamber,' and there's an enforcer on the ice, trying to lay you out, that's another thing."

At the hearing Campbell refused to discuss the anti-Semitic aspects of the case because Zeidel had absolved Shack in that regard. Zeidel echoes his thoughts about the first Shack incident when discussing the results of this one. "I should have had a lawyer at that hearing. The brass was there, but it's window dressing. In the meantime, I get four games, Shack gets three."

The denouement of Zeidel's career took place in September of 1968. He had expected to make the Philadelphia varsity once more but inexplicably was dropped from the squad in place of another veteran defenseman, Allan Stanley. Without Zeidel, the Flyers were a spirit-less, unattractive club that compiled a dismal record compared with the previous team. Larry settled in the Philadelphia area and became a stockbroker. He remains at that work to this day.

From time to time, he has been invited to play in old-timers' games. In one such contest in Madison Square Garden, Zeidel was cautioned because, as Gordie Howe put it, "He was trying too darn hard." The fire in Larry's stomach has never burned out.

Chapter 11

DAVE SCHULTZ: THE BROAD STREET BULLY

Dave Schultz was not the first free-swinging hockey hooligan nor was he the last. Yet there was something about The Hammer's style, his timing, and his arrival on the NHL scene that set him apart from the Ted Lindsays, John Fergusons, and other bad guys.

During the early 1970s, when goon hockey was in vogue, Schultz was the archetypical brawler. His mien, his volcanic temper, and his zealousness in playing the heavy made his name synonymous with ice-fighting then and to this day.

It was not uncommon to hear parents during the 1970s say to their children, "Do you want to be a hockey player — or a Dave Schultz?"

No player in NHL history more epitomized the goon, as we know the term in modern hockey history, than Dave Schultz. A sensitive, temperate and often articulate fellow away from the hockey wars, Schultz came to symbolize the truculent, often vicious side of hockey that became a major selling point during the decade of the 1970s. Schultz established his reputation as a member of the Philadelphia Flyers, although he later played for Los Angeles and Pittsburgh, before concluding his career with the Buffalo Sabres.

Schultz was a contradiction in terms in every way. He admittedly was a nonbelligerent during his teenage days as an aspiring junior hockey player. He executed a complete turnabout when he became a professional and then, after establishing himself as the ultimate NHL warrior, Schultz again altered his act and became a target rather than an assailant and finally left the league rather wimpily having exhausted his usefulness as a player.

To this day arguments rage over Schultz, his impact on the game, his value during the Flyers' two Stanley Cup victories (1974–75) and whether or not he could have succeeded in major professional hockey without his fists.

Supporters of Schultz, such as veteran Flyers broadcaster Gene Hart, long have argued that Schultz was unfairly maligned and was, in fact, a major force with the Flyers. "You must remember," says Hart, "that

Dave was a 20-goal player [1973–74] which was not a small accomplishment at that time."

Schultz's fights in some cases became classics, including decisions over John Van Boxmeer, Dale Rolfe, and Terry O'Reilly.

"Dave Schultz was unique because, more than anyone else in that decade," says Hart in his book *Score!*, "he changed the face of the game, while changing the faces of many of the game's players. He changed not only the record book, but the rule book, and he changed the thinking of most of the teams in the league. And for one of those teams, the Flyers, he created an aura and a signature unlike any other in the league's history.

"From a total lack of identity in the sixties, two players gave the Flyers character in the seventies. Bobby Clarke gave them their hard-working, tenacious, never-give-up quality, while Schultz gave them their sneering, cocky, even arrogant 'Broad Street Bullies' temperament. It was a personality akin to that of the 'Big Bad Boston Bruins,' but it was also uniquely the Flyers' own.

"Schultz's philosophy was simple: 'I'll fight anybody or do anything, but nobody's going to fool with my team.' In that sense, Dave was a leader of Freddy's [coach Shero] Philistines, the Mad Squad, the Bullies and, of course, Schultz's Army, complete with German helmets. As opposition tough guy Jerry 'King Kong' Korab once said, 'The Flyers don't want to fight you one on one: they want to fight you 19 to one.' The other side of that thinking is that no Flyer would have allowed another Flyer to be pounded into the ice, like a nail by a hammer, the way Dale Rolfe of the Rangers was hammered by Dave Schultz."

Schultz never would have been tagged as such an aggressive type had he been scouted for toughness during his early hockey days in western Canada.

"I wanted no part of the rough stuff," said Schultz, about his playing days with Swift Current. "I still recoiled from baseballs and let other guys fight my battles. I was a coward and I proved it when a brawl broke out on the ice in Flin Flon with the Bombers. I hid in the bench area. If I could have crawled under the bench I would have.

"Another time, I couldn't get to my hideout on the bench. Before I could get away from the fight one of the Bombers skated up to me and drilled me one right in the head. When I regained consciousness the referee was standing over me.

" 'Schultz,' he said, pointing to the penalty box. 'Five minutes for fighting.'

"I hadn't even gotten my gloves off and I was flat on my face and he gave me five for fighting. If that was the jungle law of hockey, I knew I wasn't going to survive long as a pacifist."

The change in Schultz's hockey persona came when he grabbed the opportunity to turn professional. His skills were, at best, modest but he was offered an opportunity and snatched the gold ring. In his auto-biography, *Hammer*, Schultz details how he went from ordinary player to a skating hellion.

"I knew," said Schultz, "that I couldn't avoid body contact al-together, so I devised a half-assed form of aggression. Hit and run like hell. It was very effective. I'd skate into the corner after the puck and if an opponent was there I'd offhandedly give him the back of my glove or toss a half-hearted punch with my glove on and get out of there so fast the other guy would hardly know who did it. At least this gave me the feel of physical contact.

"Deep down I knew that that was not enough; sooner or later I would be challenged to a face-to-face fight. It happened during a game with the Brandon Wheat Kings, another junior team from western Canada. At one point in the game I found myself on a collision course with Butch Deadmarsh, the very same Deadmarsh I would later meet on the ice at Atlanta.

"Neither of us gave an inch. Normally I would have turned away from Deadmarsh and followed the puck, but I had become a bit confi-dent as a result of my small collection of skirmishes and, instead of running from Deadmarsh, I once and for all put up my dukes. The mere act of getting into fighting position gave me goose pimples. I felt like a wetnose soldier about to face his first hail of bullets. I was scared, to be sure, but I also was experiencing a hostile form of ecstasy that I wanted to savour as long as possible.

"Before Deadmarsh lifted a finger I swung my fist around and rammed it directly into his face. For a split second I didn't know what to do. To be honest, the sensation of my knuckles colliding with his cheek made me want to jump for joy. Then I felt awkward about what I had done, and a little ashamed."

Having perfected a fighting formula Schultz built on it and with every KO he became more notorious and — not so coincidentally — feared.

Dave was the right man in the right place at the right time. The NHL was undergoing rapid expansion, which created a need for players. All the skilled positions were filled quickly, so expansion teams did the natural thing and rounded out their squads with ruffians.

Ironically, the Flyers were one of the last teams to accept the trend. They had been relatively small in stature from their inception in 1967 until the start of the 1970s. They had been physically humiliated by the two-fisted Plager brothers and Noel Picard of the St. Louis Blues, not to mention the Big Bad Bruins whose bullies included Ted Green, Wayne Cashman, John McKenzie, Derek Sanderson, and Don Awrey. By the start of the 1970s, Flyers owner Ed Snider had had it with "soft" hockey players. He made a simple and rather obvious decision to fight fire with fire. If the Flyers were going to lose they would go down swinging.

Schultz was ready for the NHL precisely when Snider's new order was being formulated. For a short time Dave was tempted to jump to the rival World Hockey Association and actually attended a press conference held by the New York Raiders, for whom he supposedly would play. But the Snider offer prevailed and the Flyers never were the same after that.

"When the Flyers told me I had made the big team in September 1972," said Schultz, "I was truly shocked. My father was convinced for years that I would reach the National Hockey League; not only that, but that I would stay there and become a prominent personality in the sport.

"I had no problem discerning that the Flyers of 1972–73 would accent sock over style. The club's schedule brochure reemphasized the point, asking 'CAN THE MEAN MACHINE CRUNCH THIS BUNCH?' We were The Mean Machine and the rest of the NHL teams represented the bunch we were to crunch.

"The philosophy was made evident from training camp to the opening of the season. Freddie Shero, in his second season coaching Philadelphia, constantly harped on the necessity of hitting. Over and over again, he would tell us to finish our checks, which meant checking the opposition even if he didn't have the puck and taking the enemy out at every turn. 'Use the body' was a theme that was repeated so often it became permanently etched in the brain. What was less articulated but still understood was that we were never — but never! — to turn the other cheek if we were attacked by the enemy."

Quite the contrary; the new Flyers believed in the pre-emptive strike: Belt them first and let the opposition worry about whether it has the guts to counterattack. The philosophy stemmed from Shero, who had been a boxer himself, as well as a tough defenseman in the NHL and the minors. When Freddie originally became a minor league coach he invariably cultivated a fighting team, and the Flyers certainly would be no different. Now, for a change, Philadelphia had the personnel. Bob Kelly was complemented by Barry Ashbee, Bobby Clarke, and Don Saleski, not to mention Ed Van Impe, one of the most competent stickmen ever to step onto an NHL rink; Wayne Hillman, a hard-bitten pro; and goalie Doug Favell, who was a slasher.

In no time at all, Schultz had become internationally known for better or worse.

"I recall a luncheon before the Flyers were to play the Russians," says Hart, "and all of the players were introduced and asked to stand. More than any other Flyer, except perhaps Bobby Clarke, the Soviet players all strained to see for themselves what this legendary bad man, Dave Schultz, looked like."

"Of all the moments I savour," says Schultz, "the one that remains the most satisfying occurred on May 18, 1974, when we defeated the Boston Bruins to win the Stanley Cup. I had come out of the regular season with a respectable total of 20 goals and the conviction that the best was yet to come. More than that, I had inherited a following: The shy kid from Rosetown, Saskatchewan had become a civic hero. [Philadelphia] mayor Frank Rizzo presented us with the keys to the city and a Stanley Cup party was held in our honour.

"On Saturday, August 24, 1974, Rosetown gave me a 'Dave Schultz Day,' starting with a Schultz breakfast at the Legion Hall, a Flyers show and hockey highlights at the Rosetown Theatre, Schultz Street Games, and finally a Schultz Burger and Drink to round out the afternoon. In the evening the Rosetown Chamber of Commerce held a Schultzfest and a Schultz Dance at the arena."

The Hammer's popularity — not to mention his notoriety — lasted as long as the Flyers were on top. They won the Stanley Cup a second time in 1975 and reached the finals in 1976. By this time, Schultz had become the target of every aspiring tough guy who entered the NHL. Even normally nonbelligerent players took on Schultz.

Clearly, the most significant turnabout in his career came during the 1976 Stanley Cup finals. Schultz's intimidation tactics were defused by tough Montreal performers like Larry Robinson. The Flyers lost in four straight games and management soon came to regard Schultz as a liability. He was traded to Los Angeles in 1976 and as a member of the Kings was like a fish out of water. Without his henchmen, "Hound" Kelly, Moose Dupont, and "Big Bird" Saleski, Schultz suddenly looked (and acted) a lot less tough than he did as a Flyer.

He was badly beaten up by the Flyers' Paul Holmgren in his return to Philadelphia. And from that point on, his ferocity diminished. The Kings unloaded him to Pittsburgh and he concluded his career with Buffalo in 1979–80. In his autobiography, Schultz confessed that by the twilight of his career the intimidator became the intimidated.

Chapter 12

DAVE "TIGER" WILLIAMS: THE TASMANIAN DEVIL ON ICE

Perhaps the most telling words about Dave "Tiger" Williams came from the lips of Islanders superstar Mike Bossy. An exquisitely clean player, Bossy was relentlessly pursued by Williams throughout the early 1980s.

Bossy: "Tiger was Tiger. He taunted me, threw elbows at me, worked, cross-checked and punched me."

To hockey purists like Bossy, Williams represented everything evil about hockey. He was a hatchetman; he would whack you from behind, spear and intimidate in every possible way to win a hockey game. Considering his size (5'11", 185 pounds), Williams was gambling with dismemberment. But throughout his career he remained thoroughly indomitable and indefatigable. He also set an NHL record for penalties (3,966 minutes) over a career that spanned 14 seasons.

Williams had a piranha-like quality about him. He would just as soon impale you with his stick as needle you with his mouth. Not surprisingly, Williams was the centrepiece of one of the most vicious playoff series in modern NHL annals, the 1978 confrontation between the Maple Leafs and Islanders. Led by Williams, Jerry Butler, and Dan Maloney, the Maple Leafs bludgeoned the more artistic New Yorkers at every turn. And when the Torontonians weren't hitting them with their bodies and sticks, they withered them with their mouths. Tiger was high man on the soapbox. Typical was his observation about the enemy after the series was tied at two apiece.

"You know the Islanders are crying," Williams said. "They know that if we hit them, we'll beat them. I don't go around crying about getting hit or getting stuck. The only guys who don't cry on their team are their best players, Bryan Trottier and Clark Gillies. The rest of them are a bunch of fairies, yelling it's tough and rough and things like that."

Bossy, with unusual candour, allowed that Williams was talking specifically about him. In his autobiography, *Boss*, Bossy admitted that

Williams was fingering him in particular. "Williams was talking about me and as I look back, he was right," said Bossy. "I wasn't complaining, but I was intimidated. I always was afraid of playing against people who had a total disregard for others. Williams couldn't have cared less if he broke my neck."

It didn't hurt that Williams played under coaches who favoured goon hockey, especially Roger Neilson, who was behind the bench during the 1978 Toronto–Islander series as well as the 1982 playoffs with Vancouver. It was in 1982 that the Williams-led Canucks marauded through the playoffs, letting blood at every turn. In the semi-finals, featuring Vancouver and Chicago, the Canucks simply butchered the Blackhawks in the decisive final game to win the series.

Williams was more than a goon. He owned modest offensive skills that occasionally produced a timely goal, but he had no illusions about his qualities.

"Nobody had to tell me that I wasn't a Lafleur or a Bobby Orr," he said. "I knew I would never be idolized. I didn't have the stuff it required. But I knew I could impress the fans in other ways. I knew I would convince them I was doing all I could on their behalf. No fan could say that 'Williams is stealing the money they pay him.' "

The feeling of some NHL scouts is that the toughest hockey players come from the Canadian West where they endure bitter cold, long bus rides, and a heritage of robust frontier-style hockey. Tiger's feistiness came by way of his father, a Welshman who raised him in Weyburn, Saskatchewan.

"Dad spent $10 on each of us boys to enroll us in hockey and then about $150 on equipment and he wasn't gonna see it go to waste," said the Tiger. "You had to work your ass off for him. If you came home and didn't win because you didn't try, he'd scream his head off. I was afraid not to try. If I tried and lost, it was bad, but not as bad as when I didn't try. He did so much for me, he believed in me so goddamn much that I just couldn't hurt him."

"David had to work for all he got," said his dad, "Taffy" Williams. "They all did. I always believed you came into life with nothing, but in between you owe it something. I always told the boys that anybody can be a loser if they don't try but, with a little effort, you can be a winner. When David was about six, he played goal and if his team wasn't winning, he'd carry the puck up the ice himself and try to score. That's when he got the name Tiger. He certainly was that. One time he and his older brother Len had an argument at the supper table. Len was refereeing a game David was playing in later that night. David said that if Len gave him a penalty, he'd flatten him. Naturally, Len gave him a penalty. And, sure enough, David flattened him."

Writing in *The Canadian Magazine*, author Earl McRae prodded Williams into an enlightening reflection about his family's influence.

"Len was tough," said Williams. "I was lucky. He's the only guy who ever beat me up, who ever could. That's why I levelled that teacher in high school. Len always said, 'When they start pushing, you start levelling.' Well, he pushed and I levelled. Geez, I had more fights off the ice growing up, it'd make Al Capone's days look like a fairy tale.

"My dad used to do some boxing in the old country but it was Hugh, my oldest brother — I think it started with Hugh. He had an accent when he first came over, a little guy, and the other kids bugged him, eh? Made fun of his accent, picked on him. So Dad, he taught Hugh how to box. This boxing club, eh? Hugh was small but quick. He got real good. Anyway, there was always boxing around the house. Mom and Dad would go out and us kids would shove back the chairs and things, get out the gloves and go to it.

"Morgan, my kid brother, he was a Canadian gold medallist fighter, the best in the country in his weight. A real quiet gentleman kind of guy, too, nothing like me. Funny, eh? All my brothers were Saskatchewan champs at one time. Except me. I played hockey. I could have been, but I played hockey. But I showed them I could be by doing it in hockey. Yeah, I think that's probably it. Sure. That's it."

Williams had instant impact on the NHL following his three-year stint with Swift Current in the Western Canada Junior League. He was drafted in the second round by the Maple Leafs and racked up 187 penalty minutes in only 42 games' work. By the time his fourth season rolled around, Tiger was regularly breaking the 300-penalty-minutes-per-season barrier.

McRae once observed that Tiger's nose "looks like a crunched beer can."

In fact, by the time Williams was twenty-one his nose had been broken eight times.

Williams never feared a foe or a challenge. "There's the risk of getting hurt in any walk of life," he said. "You could get killed anytime; you could get run over by a streetcar. But sooner or later you gotta cross that street.

"I don't really excel in any department. I am mainly average. But I feel there's not too many guys in the whole league who were in better condition than I am. And I'm mentally strong. I can keep the same attitude through 80 games and during the playoffs."

When Tiger turned twenty-four, he had become one of the league's most penalized players, as well as one of its most vocal. Once in a preliminary playoff round against Pittsburgh, Williams announced after one game that the Penguins were "done like dinner" and eventually he was right, as Toronto beat them. Against the Islanders in the quarterfinals with the games tied at three, he said the Islanders were not only "done like dinner," but they were "burnt toast." Then he added that they were "so far out in left field they're beyond hand-grenade range." It was typically brash and annoyed some teammates who feared that Williams would antagonize the Islanders to a greater effort and, ultimately, help them win the series. But nobody was going to button the Tiger's lip. He continued yapping and, guess what, Toronto won the series in sudden-death overtime of the seventh game.

Williams's career included stops in Toronto, Vancouver, Detroit, Los Angeles, and Hartford. His last spate of good hockey was played in Los Angeles where the Kings found his truculence to their advantage.

"Basically we picked him up as playoff insurance," said then King coach Pat Quinn. "We wanted an experienced player who could help us in the playoffs. The guy is a competitive marvel. In his own way he knows what he can do. L.A. seems to be a tough town for guys to keep their minds on their business, but Tiger doesn't have any problem."

Williams retired in 1988 but still plays amateur hockey in British Columbia — a lot milder, we might add.

Chapter 13

JOHN FERGUSON: THE ORIGINAL ENFORCER

Until John Ferguson arrived on the NHL scene in 1963 there had not been what came to be known as an "enforcer" in the NHL.

Naturally, there had been an endless list of tough hockey players, but no one who was specifically designated as a protector of more docile teammates.

Ferguson was a first; and a very significant one at that.

He was promoted from the Cleveland Barons of the American League primarily as a bodyguard for Canadiens centre (and captain) Jean Beliveau. This decision was made by the Habs' high command specifically because Beliveau had been mauled during the 1961 Stanley Cup round by the Chicago Blackhawks. The captain needed protection and after a long search the Canadiens discovered Ferguson in the AHL.

Ferguson was a mean-spirited youngster out of Vancouver who had made his way along the pro hockey route from Fort Wayne to Cleveland. With the Barons he studied under Fred Glover, a former NHL player notorious for his tenacity and lack of etiquette on ice.

"I learned just by watching Glover in action," says Ferguson. "He was the greatest competitor I've ever seen. Nothing would stop him. For example, even when he was badly hurt, he still insisted on getting back into action. He'd have himself taped up from head to foot, yet he would somehow manage to return to the ice because he loved hockey so much.

"Freddie fought a lot, and he occasionally lost. I saw him get whipped worse in fist fights than any guy I've ever seen; but two minutes later Freddie would be up and at it, going after the same guy who had beaten him up. Just being around Glover was enough to pick up another guy's spirits."

At first the Canadiens had no idea whether Ferguson would make the big club, but he already had his personal strategy charted at training camp.

"The first thing I did," said Fergy, "when we started scrimmaging was to run into as many opponents as possible. That seemed to please coach Toe Blake, and I managed to survive every cut in the squad. I finally learned that I had made the team."

Ferguson not only made the Canadiens varsity on the first try, he emerged as a scoring threat as well as a guardian of Beliveau, and other smaller Canadiens.

In his first NHL game, at Boston Garden, he challenged Ted Green, then the league's most fearsome fighter, and outpointed the Bruin heavyweight.

The decision over Green was no fluke. Ferguson would battle *any* opponent who threatened his teammates and the results were eminently positive. Beliveau's career was rejuvenated and the Canadiens won Stanley Cups in 1965 and 1966. Ferguson, it should be noted, played an important function both as an offensive catalyst and as a deterrent to those who would trifle with Beliveau and company.

One of the most telling examples of Ferguson-the-fighter at work took place in April 1968 when the Canadiens met Bobby Orr and the Big Bad Bruins in the playoffs.

"You watch the Bruin tough guys," said one newsman, "go after the smaller Montrealers early in the game, soften 'em up, and then you'll see the game turn in Boston's favour."

It was an interesting proposition, and not without its merits. Fortified with such bombers as Green, Don Awrey, Eddie Shack, and Johnny McKenzie, the Bruins had perhaps the meanest, toughest team in hockey. Green and McKenzie had led a successful war against the Rangers during the season and paced the Beantowners to a clear-cut margin over their New York foes. "Intimidation" was the secret word and a workable strategy directed against Montreal, but it didn't account for Ferguson.

Early in the game Ferguson seemed to detect the Bruins' strategy on his radarscope and went after Green. Johnny's battle plan was a study in logic. With one hand he grabbed Green's jersey and lifted it high over the Boston player's head so that he was both blinded and partly handcuffed. And with the other hand, Ferguson pummelled Green about the head until there was little doubt that the Montrealer had scored a decisive victory over a man who rarely lost fights.

Just how decisive the victory was soon became evident. The Bruins turned pussycats and, with their tails between their legs, crept out of the series in four straight games. While Ferguson didn't exactly win the round for the Habs, he turned the psychological lever in Montreal's direction and the Canadiens roared on to win yet another Stanley Cup.

When he was playing for Cleveland, it was not uncommon for Johnny to take on more than one opponent. Once he was confronted by Gary Collins of the Pittsburgh club. "I suppose you think you're tough," Collins challenged Ferguson.

"Tough enough to handle you," Ferguson replied and then hauled off and belted Collins. The force of the blow sent both men sprawling through an open door, whereupon Bob Bailey, another Pittsburgh player, threw himself on Ferguson.

Soon both benches cleared and a gala brawl took place that eventually resulted in $610 in fines. Such episodes as the Collins and Green fights symbolized Ferguson's philosophy: "It's a question of honour," John explained. "Not for me . . . for everybody on the team. It makes me sick to see people standing around and doing nothing when a guy is taking a lacing. What I mean is, if you let a team push you around they'll push you hard. Fight back and maybe they aren't too anxious to test you. Let 'em know you're there, that you're ready, and maybe they'll respect you."

Ferguson's will to win was far above the norm, and he wasn't bashful talking about his fighting ability.

"I don't know why they bleed so much when I hit them," he once said. "It's been like that since I was a kid. Maybe it's because of these knuckles."

During the 1965 playoffs, Fergy collided with Eric Nesterenko of the Chicago Blackhawks — notorious for his flying elbows. Ferguson tossed one punch that flattened Nesterenko. The result was similar to the Green incident. Chicago lost heart after that, and the Canadiens roared on to win the Cup.

The case of Ferguson and other ruffians inspires a question — how did a hockey fighter get that way? In his case the answer was as direct as one of his punches. When John was a kid growing up in Vancouver, he got a job as stickboy for the Vancouver Canucks (then of the Western Hockey League). One night the Canucks were playing the Edmonton Flyers and high-scoring Phil Maloney, Vancouver's little centre, became embroiled in a fight with Edmonton's big, tough defenseman, Larry Zeidel. It all happened in front of Fergy at the Vancouver bench.

"Zeidel sneaked up on him from behind," said Fergy. "He just killed Maloney. Phil almost lost an eye. I stood there and looked at the other players on that Vancouver team. Not one guy went to help. I hated that whole team. I made up my mind that if I ever became a hockey player, I'd never stand by and watch something like that happen to one of my teammates."

Sure enough, Ferguson eventually graduated to Cleveland where he found himself face-to-face with Zeidel, who played for Hershey. Unaware of Fergy's feelings, Zeidel was taken aback when John vaulted the boards, headed straight for him, and then flailed him with punches. "Yeah," said Ferguson, "I gave him a few for Phil."

Once up with the Canadiens, Fergy appeared to be anxious to prove himself. In his exuberance he wound up collecting an excessive amount of penalties — 125 minutes in his rookie year (Note: they only played 70 games in those days) — but there was little management could do about it. "Asking Ferguson to stop being aggressive is like asking a hockey player to stop playing the game," said general manager Sam Pollock. "It never crossed our minds. But we did want him to stop getting silly penalties late in the game. What's the good of a hooking penalty in the other team's end of the rink late in the game? All it could do was hurt us."

Fergy got the word but his penalty minutes didn't diminish. On the contrary, they went up — 156, 153, and a league-leading 177. Coach Blake never encouraged Fergy to chase down any particular opponent but John admits he received oblique bits of advice from his former bench boss: "He'd say quietly," Ferguson explained, " 'you'd better go out there and straighten that guy out.' I knew what he meant."

Although Fergy's fight-winning record was clean, he had suffered corollary damage in some of his clashes. Once in Boston he kayoed Ed Westfall of the Bruins with a punch, but when Westfall hit the ice, his flying skates caught Fergy on the thumb and cut his tendon.

"There was blood all over the place," John remembered. "The thumb seemed to be hanging by the skin, but I didn't think too much of it. Everything was going so good until then."

Little did he know at the time that his hockey career very nearly ended. But doctors knew he was in trouble and rushed him to the hospital for emergency surgery. "If the doctor hadn't operated immediately," said Ferguson, "I guess I'd have lost the thumb." Then he paused and added, "But I didn't lose the fight. If I did, how come Westfall had all that snow on his back?"

After a clash with Doug Mohns of Chicago, scratches appeared on Fergy's face the following morning — from the top of his right cheek to the corner of his mouth. Once again, John was quick to point out that the scratch marks had nothing to do with the decision. "He's not a fighter," Fergy insisted, "he's a scratcher. I'd sure hate to be in the ring if that so-and-so [writer who said that Mohns won the bout] was a boxing judge. And I'll bet that Mohns has a pretty good shiner this morning."

The majority of John's emphatic victories occurred in fights on the road. Early in the 1967–68 season he clearly decisioned New York's Reg Fleming at Madison Square Garden, setting the stage for an equally emphatic Montreal win. "There's not much point in throwing a punch or two at home," Fergy noted. "But a scrap often helps the team on the road. I like the guys to know I'm right behind them when the game gets rough. I think it gives some of our lighter players a lift." In the Stanley Cup finals against St. Louis in May 1968, he floored Barclay Plager with one punch. "He must have had a hard head," said Ferguson, "because I hurt my hand."

Some of Ferguson's bouts — over Eric Nesterenko, Bobby Hull, and Ted Green — became more legendary than Montreal victories. The wins over Nesterenko and Green gave the Canadiens such a psychological lift, they went on to win championships. He showed his irreverence for Hull by going after the Chicago Golden Boy, although Hull was wearing a faceguard to protect a broken jaw. Fergy continued to excel through the end of the 1960s and into the next decade. His success could be measured in Stanley Cup rings. By 1970 he had four and was taking aim at a fifth.

He concluded his career in the 1970–71 season still working alongside Beliveau and protecting his leader. It was rather appropriate that Ferguson concluded his turbulent career with a Stanley Cup win in 1971, his fifth championship club.

As often happens when a team wins the Stanley Cup, opponents look to the champions and attempt to copy their formula for success. Thus, at the start of the 1970s, as the NHL continued to expand, general managers examined the Habs and quickly grasped the significance of an ice cop like Ferguson; how well he did his job and what a player like him would mean to their teams.

Thus, the era of the goon dawned on the NHL. In no time at all other clubs were pursuing and signing tough guys and by 1974 the Broad Street Bullies, otherwise known as the Philadelphia Flyers, became the first expansion team to win the Stanley Cup.

Chapter 14

THE TRAGEDY OF DWIGHT SCHOFIELD

About a year or so after Dwight Schofield's retirement from hockey, he phoned me to suggest a literary collaboration of some kind. He sounded clearly disturbed by his reputation as a bad guy of hockey and wanted to set the record straight. I told him that it would be extremely difficult "to sell" a Schofield book but it would depend in large part on what he had to say. I asked him to tape as much as he could and then send me a transcript. What we got out of it was considerably less than book material but a rather sensitive look at an athlete who reflectively wished that his career could have gone in another direction.

We agreed that we would try to sell Schofield's story as a magazine piece, which meant that two of his targets, Jacques Demers and Bryan Murray, would have the right of rebuttal. Which they did.

Schofield's story never even made it in magazine form, but I did eventually do a column on him in The Hockey News. His is a simple tale of a "role player" retroactively lamenting his role.

Were Dwight Schofield reincarnated as an eighteen-year-old preparing for a big-league career in a fighting-reduced, goonless NHL of the 1990s, he hardly would resemble the skating rhino who marauded for the Blues and Capitals in the 1980s.

"When I started playing the game," muses Schofield, now a St. Louis insurance salesman, "I was a total finesse player. I wouldn't hit anyone if I was paid. All I would do was go out and throw a million moves, score a million goals, and didn't want anything to do with the rough stuff."

Yet the very "rough stuff" Schofield disdained as a youth eventually became his ticket to the bigs. He made his NHL debut with the Red Wings in 1976–77, had a cup of coffee with the Canadiens in 1982–83, spent two years (1983–85) with the Blues, and moved on to Washington (1985–86), Pittsburgh (1986–87), and finally Winnipeg in 1987–88.

Like hockey's archetypical enforcer, Dave "Hammer" Schultz, Schofield underwent a slow metamorphosis from pussycat to panther. Now an articulate, reflective ex-hockey player, Dwight calmly analyzes the transformation from the comfort of his insurance office.

"As a youngster, I was accused of playing hockey like a butterfly by my old man," he chuckles. "I had an older brother who I was always being compared to by my dad. He'd tell me I should stop being such a wimp and be like my older brother and be a tough 'bad boy.' "

Schofield insists that he had no intentions of taking his father's advice. Finesse hockey was his forte and he stuck to that style as he climbed the teenage ladder in his native Massachusetts.

"Despite the fact that I liked sticking to hockey — the fun part of the game — I occasionally had to fight," he remembers, "and with my size [6'3", 195 pounds] I did pretty well. I didn't look for trouble but people took note of the way I fought and all of a sudden they expected me to do it more and more."

Deciding that his hockey future could best be pursued in Canada, Schofield left his Rhode Island private school at age sixteen and moved to Toronto and then London, Ontario where he played two Ontario Hockey Association seasons with the Knights. He totalled 245 penalty minutes and a year later got his first taste of the NHL in Detroit, scoring a goal and receiving one penalty in three games.

The Red Wings were so impressed they demoted Dwight to Kalamazoo (IHL) from where he moved to Kansas City (IHL), back to Kalamazoo, Fort Wayne, Dayton, Tulsa, Milwaukee, and Nova Scotia before he got his major break with the Blues in 1983. Jacques Demers was the coach, Ron Caron the manager, and Harry Ornest the owner of a St. Louis team that was nearly moved to Saskatoon.

Schofield had another encounter with Demers, this time after Jacques had left St. Louis to become coach of the Red Wings. Dwight was uncertain about his future at the time and had not been formally invited to any NHL training camp when he received a phone call from his ex-coach.

"Jacques said he wanted me to do him a favour," Schofield remembers. "He had two of his tough guys in the doghouse and wanted to shit can on them. He wanted me to take their place. I said sure and went to camp. As soon as I got there, Demers gave me the old spiel, 'Oh, I'm so glad to have you,' and made it seem like he was high on me.

"On top of that, I had a good camp, got some points, played tough, had some fights and when it was over I found out that the two tough guys who had been in the doghouse were back in Jacques's good books. Then he had the audacity to call me in and say he really didn't have much use for me and I should go to their farm team. I go to help the guy out and as soon as I'm not needed, it's like, f—— you! It was a slap in the face; very typical of the every-man-for-himself attitude."

Although Schofield often sounds bitter, he also is grateful that he did get an opportunity to play big-league hockey. It also is clear that he never really adapted to the tough-guy role in which he felt obliged to adjust in order to remain an NHLer.

"Despite the fact that I was fighting and for all outward appearances appeared to do well, it really took a serious toll on me on the inside because I was unemotionally tough. I had trouble sleeping at night thinking about big games that were coming up and all the fights that I might have to have despite the fact I really wasn't into it."

After two seasons with the Blues, Schofield was left unprotected in the 1985 waiver draft, whereupon he was claimed by Washington and played 50 games for the Capitals in 1985–86. He went from the gregarious Demers to the more serious Bryan Murray.

"Bryan was all business," Schofield remembers. "He didn't believe in having a whole lot of fun. Talk about a regimented outfit and red tape, you should see the Capitals. They would issue a news release for you to take a shit; or file an official report on the incident.

"For all his faults, Demers was a good-hearted guy. Murray basically didn't give a shit about the players, didn't worry about how they felt. He said my only purpose was to neutralize Philadelphia. I got pissed off and had countless meetings, saying I can play. They had no respect for my feelings whatsoever. In practice I'd be made to feel like a total piece of shit."

Interestingly, one of Schofield's favourite coaches was ex-Maple Leafs leader John Brophy, for whom Dwight played when he was in the AHL. Like Dwight, Brophy had been a brawler in his heyday and Schofield would look at the coach and see some of himself in the white-thatched man.

"What's particularly interesting about John Brophy and myself," Schofield explains, "is the fact that we were two extremely volatile people with tempers that won't quit. A lot of times we had incidents that almost had us going at it with our fists."

Among the more memorable episodes was the time Brophy, unhappy over Dwight's play, demanded Schofield leave the bench during a game at Hershey and then refused to allow Dwight to get on the team bus. Brophy insisted that he walk back to the hotel in Hershey while the rest of the team took the bus to Baltimore two and a half hours away.

"Brophy would go off the deep end every so often," Schofield adds, "particularly after we'd lose big games. Once he busted a window on the bus and got into a fight with the bus driver. Another time he threw his wristwatch down on the floor and jumped up and down doing a flamenco dance on it and busted it into a million pieces.

"Then there was the time we checked into a hotel in Portland, Maine, only to be told by a very heavy female desk clerk that all the rooms had been booked. Brophy shouted that he hoped the hotel burned down. The heavy lady yelled back, 'If it burns down, it'll have to be with me in it.' Brophy thought for a second and said, 'Well, if it does, we'll be eating roast pork for two months straight.' "

Schofield swings at his ex-bosses as freely as he did at opponents and, in some cases, those who have coached him have been just as vigorous in swinging back. Demers, for example, hardly agrees with Dwight's accusations and offers his own interpretation of their relationship.

"He's two-faced," Demers charges, "and not being honest. I never told him I wanted him to go out and fight but I did tell him that I wanted him to be the tough guy or enforcer. As far as my favouring players is concerned, there's not a coach around who won't take care of his better players. I took care of players who worked hard and produced."

After hearing Schofield's assertions, Demers insists that Dwight is simply engaging in some personal revisionist history that is not consistent with the facts as he remembers them.

"As far as his experience with the Red Wings, it was Schofield who called several times and wanted a tryout — without a contract. He knew where he stood. We offered him a minor league contract and he didn't want it. My GM didn't even want him."

"Demers told me that my only job from that point on was going to be as a fighter," Schofield recalls. "They said they were going to make me [from a defenseman] into a wing so I could fight and extend my career. Otherwise, they said, I wouldn't be able to continue to play."

But he also thought he had better obey the master if he was going to survive in the majors. And, in fact, Dwight played 70 games for St. Louis in 1983–84, tallied 4–10–14 and 219 penalty minutes. It was the beginning of the Demers era with the Blues, one in which Jacques-Be-Nimble would charm the city and its fans.

"Jacques was a helluva guy," says Schofield. "He really liked people and wanted people to like him but in the heat of the battle, he could be a real prick. He had this serious need to be the big man, a real hero. He used to like to shit on people when he thought he could, to make himself look like a real big man.

"I was the kind of guy he figured he could shit on and get away with it because I was a marginal player who was low man on the totem pole. By contrast, with a guy like Bernie Federko Jacques was scared shitless of laying down the law, thinking he'd get fired if he did."

Once Demers noticed that Schofield didn't have a tie at the St. Louis airport prior to a trip to Minnesota. Dwight was left behind because of the sartorial indiscretion. "Another time," Schofield continues, "he saw me laughing in the dressing room during a game we were losing badly. He called a meeting before we went out on the ice and told me before the rest of the players, 'Schoie, if I ever see you laughing again when we're losing, I'll belt you right in the mouth.' I figured that he'd shit in his drawers if I ever made like I was going to come at him." Schofield did plenty of fighting for Demers over two seasons. During his second year with the Blues (1984–85), Dwight played 43 games and amassed 184 penalty minutes.

Schofield asserts that enforcers such as himself were like little slaves on the bottom of the totem pole. The superstars were, not surprisingly, on the top.

"The Blues had [goalie] Mike Liut at the time and I'll never forget one meeting we had where everyone was supposed to voice his opinions about team problems. When we got to Mike he said, 'I know what the problem with this team is; there's no respect.' He went on to say that the guys who had been there for four or five years own the team. The guys who hadn't been there that long should kiss his and everyone else's ass who was geared that way and Demers went along with it.

"The proof is in another incident involving another star, defenseman Rob Ramage. The guy missed a plane to Calgary, so Jacques cancelled the practice just because Ramage wasn't there. Of course, if it would have been one of the lesser players, Demers would have given the guy shit up and down and gone ahead and had the practice anyway."

Schofield believes he was constantly victimized by the double standard. He remembers a summer workout before training camp began. Dwight cut teammate Dave Barr with a two-hander and Demers soon learned of the incident.

"Jacques was real pissed off and said he didn't want any more screwing around with sticks during training camp, otherwise the culprit would be in big trouble. A couple of days later Brian Sutter, who was the captain and Demers's pet, turned around and gave Craig Levie — another low man on the totem pole — a totally uncalled-for stick in the nose, breaking his beak. Not a word was said to him by Demers."

Demers was more than puzzled, if not upset, when he found out that he was receiving the wrath of Schofield.

"My question is," says Demers, "why didn't he ever tell me this right away? All he did was bitch about John Brophy telling him he only wanted him to fight. As long as I coached him, he was never asked to go beat anybody up."

As for the Ramage incident, Demers explains, "I cancelled practice because of Rob Ramage. He's one of the most disciplined players I've ever coached and if he missed the plane, there was good reason for it."

Demers makes no bones about the fact that "Schofield had a role [enforcer] to play and everybody knew it." Ditto Bryan Murray, who reflects on Dwight's verbal assault with significantly less bitterness than Demers. "Dwight was a good guy to have around the dressing room," Murray recalls, "but he was not a skill player. In order for him to stay with the Capitals he had to play a particular way; be tough and contribute to the team.

"When I got him, Schofield was near the end of his career but he got more ice time with us than any other team because I've always tried to play my hitters on a fairly regular basis."

Murray theorizes that hockey cops like Schofield suffer the misapprehension that they are more artistically gifted than others realize.

"Anyone who comes in as a tough player wants to be important. Neil Sheehy has had that kind of thinking and I said to him, 'Don't fool yourself' [into thinking you are what you are not]. That's what people like Schofield have come to grips with because, when you think of it, who wants to be accused of being a goon?"

No one, of course, will ever know whether Dwight Schofield would have been a better player in a more utopian hockey world, although he obviously thinks so. But now that the NHL is behind him, bitterness notwithstanding, he savours the fact that he beat the odds and made it to the bigs.

"Other guys got drafted high and jumped right up to the pros," he concludes. "I played seven years and didn't make it to the NHL until the age of twenty-seven. I played in scum cities, with scumball fans and broken-down buses, and got involved in riots. But when others in the same situation quit on themselves, I refused to let that happen to me. I said I should be up there and I believed it from the bottom of my heart."

Alan May battles for position in front of the Sabres' net. (Courtesy Bruce Bennett Studios.)

Alan May in a less belligerent moment. (Courtesy Bruce Bennett Studios.)

Basil McRae meets the press. (Courtesy Bruce Bennett Studios.)

McRae swerves in on the Penguins' goal. (Courtesy Bruce Bennett Studios.)

Linesman Kevin Collins calms McRae. (Courtesy Bruce Bennett Studios.)

Craig Berube drops the gloves for another encounter. (Courtesy Bruce Bennett Studios.)

Berube in full flight. (Courtesy Bruce Bennett Studios.)

Chris Nilan is as notorious for his yapping as for his fighting. (Courtesy Bruce Bennett Studios.)

Troy Crowder (left) and Tie Domi battle at Madison Square Garden. (Courtesy Bruce Bennett Studios.)

This is why Crowder (left) was pursued by the Red Wings. (Courtesy Bruce Bennett Studios.)

Ken Baumgartner is escorted to the penalty box after yet another bout. (Courtesy Bruce Bennett Studios.)

Tie Domi believes he can make it in the NHL without fighting. His performance indicates otherwise. (Courtesy Bruce Bennett Studios.)

Many consider Joe Kocur the meanest fighter in the NHL. (Courtesy Bruce Bennett Studios.)

Troy Mallette moved from the Rangers to Edmonton in the 1991 deal for Adam Graves. (Courtesy Bruce Bennett Studios.)

Bob Probert is regarded as the heavyweight champion of the NHL. (Courtesy Bruce Bennett Studios.)

Daren Kimble earned fame by sending Troy Crowder into a weak-kneed daze with a punch in the 1990–91 season. (Courtesy Bruce Bennett Studios.)

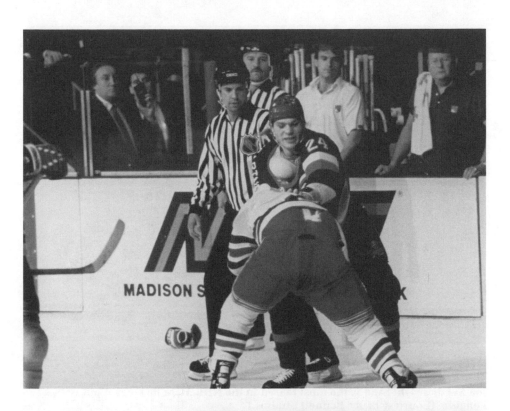

Ken Baumgartner and Tie Domi exchange punches at Nassau Coliseum. (Courtesy Bruce Bennett Studios.)

Joe Kocur's right hand is the most feared in the NHL. Here he slugs it out with a Penguin. (Courtesy Bruce Bennett Studios.)

Prelude to a bout. Quite often a hockey fight begins with a glare and an exchange of words. This is precisely what's happening here with Joe Kocur (left) and Ken Sabourin. (Courtesy Bruce Bennett Studios.)

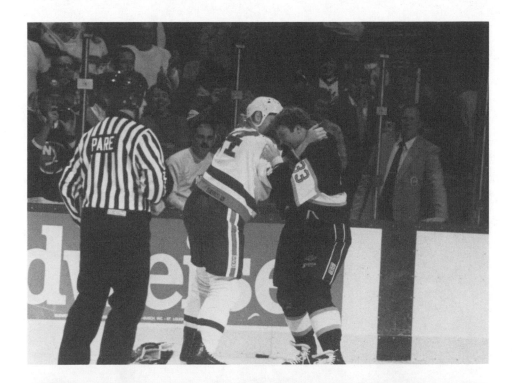

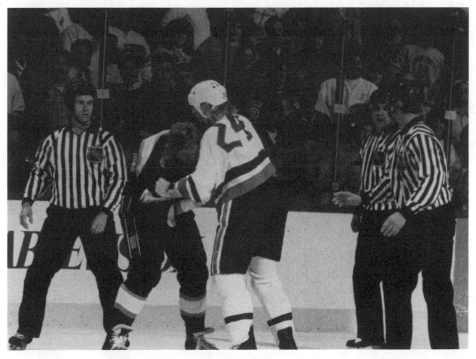

When two heavyweights such as Marty McSorley of Los Angeles and Ken Baumgartner of the Islanders trade punches, it's especially interesting. Both are intellects and their respective team player representatives. (Courtesy Bruce Bennett Studios.)

Some bad boys, such as the Islanders' Mick Vukota, will use a wrestling toss when appropriate. (Courtesy Bruce Bennett Studios.)

An old fighting warhorse, Dave Brown of the Flyers (left) never seems to tire of fisticuffs. (Courtesy Bruce Bennett Studios.)

IV

THE CONTEMPORARY ERA

Chapter 15

SANDY VIGILANTE: ARCHIVIST OF SOCK

A few years ago the NHL actually considered the abolition of fisticuffs in their hockey games. For Sandy Vigilante, the world rattled on its axis. "My life," says Vigilante, a Nutley, New Jersey postman, "is hockey fights. When I see two guys square off on the ice, I go crazy. Blood rushes to my head, my heart pounds like it'll beat through my chest. If the NHL had eliminated fighting, I don't know what I would have done."

Vigilante, America's foremost curator of hockey fights, was spared desperate measures when the NHL passed some wimpy legislation that did almost nothing to cramp the livelihood of the sports professional head-pounders. With more than 200 hours videotaped NHL gore already meticulously filed and indexed, Vigilante zealously immersed himself in the 1991–92 season. "Over the years, we've had a number of beauties," he raves with all the enthusiasm of Andrew Sarris at a Kathleen Turner film festival. "One of the best in 1986–87 was Kevin Maguire, the Leafs' new tough kid, clobbering Shane Churla of the Whalers. Both had been brought up from the minors specifically to protect teammates; when they went at it, you had a Class A bout and some dandy video."

The Maguire–Churla bout pushed the number of fights in Vigilante's collection over a thousand. The breadth of his video archives make fellow collectors, like Mark Topaz of Rockaway, in Queens, New York, revere Vigilante as "the godfather" of taped hockey fights. In fact, Vigilante is so widely respected that columnist Marc Horton of the Edmonton *Journal* once asked Vigilante for a player-by-player analysis of the Oilers.

"I got into this in '72, before VCRs," Sandy recalls. "I kept a detailed list of every fight in every hockey game I saw at the Garden or Nassau Coliseum. I'd research the out-of-town games at the library. When VCRs came out it opened a whole new world for me. I took a portable TV to games so I could watch two games at once. Meanwhile, my machine at home would be taping a Flyers game."

Vigilante turns downright sentimental rhapsodizing about the halcyon days of Philly's Broad Street Bullies. "Hey," he exclaims passionately, "the Flyers from '73–'74 to '78–'79 was classic stuff. Dave Schultz is one of the all-timers." Of course, you can reach even further for good old days. "They talk about violence today," scoffs Vigilante. "I've got a film of a Montreal–Rangers game in 1950 with a five-on-one where everybody's swinging away — with their sticks."

Vigilante's all-time favourite slugger is the late Bob Gassoff, a skating Mike Tyson of the 1970s. Among the current swingers he savours are the Flyers' Rick Tocchet and the Leafs' Wendel Clark, who both score goals as well as TKOs. "Those two had as good a fight as any you'll ever see. They went toe-to-toe at Maple Leaf Gardens once; neither gave an inch. Just beautiful!"

The NHL doesn't exactly share Vigilante's aesthetic sensibility. League officials insist that hockey fight film vendors — don't laugh, this is growing into a cottage industry — violate the NHL copyright. Once, the NHL's legal counsel, Gil Stein, wrote to *The Hockey News* to warn the weekly publication against running fight video ads. But up to four such classifieds continued to pop up each issue.

Vigilante insists he's above the fracas. "Me, I don't sell," he asserts. "The NHL is after people who started by getting some of my stuff. Then they started making some of their own and gave pure collectors like me a bad name. I only trade; I just want to get past fights that I haven't seen. If someone offered me a million dollars for all my fights, I'd kick 'em in the ass and tell 'em to get outta my house."

The pure passion that consumes Vigilante during a good NHL bout is best measured by his reaction when he unexpectedly misses punches being thrown. He was once traumatized while watching a Bruins–Canadiens playoff game on TV when a brawl erupted between John Wensink and Mario Tremblay. "The rink was packed," Sandy recalls, "and when they started swinging, people got up and blocked the camera. I got so mad I put my hand through a door and tore it off its hinges. After that, I went over to my bed and flipped it upside down. I forgot that my friend was sitting on it.

"I'll tell you how devoted I am," he elaborates. "I had a date over and instead of background music, I had an Islander game on the radio. A fight started just as we were getting hot and heavy. I said, 'Hold on a minute, I gotta hear this.' She didn't have much choice."

Clearly, we are talking about a higher love.

Chapter 16

THE HATED SUPERSTARS

The most hated superior player in National Hockey League history was Hall of Famer Eddie Shore. He intimidated foes for more than a decade and suffered at least one serious threat on his own life which, fortunately, was thwarted at the eleventh hour. Shore was so consummately loathed that late in his career, after his once-awesome strength had been weakened somewhat, the enemy sought revenge.

One night Shore made the mistake of flattening young, fiery Phil Watson of the New York Rangers. The Shore error was in committing his assault in the vicinity of Murray (Muzz) Patrick, Watson's teammate, who also was the heavyweight (boxing) champion of Canada. Patrick's one-two kayo punch was still ringing in Shore's ears years later.

There have been reasonable facsimiles of Shore in the NHL since then, although none as hated. Toronto's Bashin' Bill Barilko was nearly run out of the league by Rangers' general manager Frank Boucher after the oft-despised (by opponents) Barilko broke the collarbone of New York forward Jack McLeod. Then there was Detroit's aptly named "Terrible" Ted Lindsay, who once carved the Bruins' "Wild Bill" Ezinicki for 19 stitches in one of the bloodiest one-on-ones east of the Chicago stockyards.

Times have not changed in the NHL — only the names. And while there may not be a superstar who was so consistently disliked for his ferocity, yet intensely admired for his ability, as Shore, there are several notables who have managed, for an assortment of reasons, to earn their niche on the NHL hate parade, even the men between the pipes.

One of them was Derek Sanderson, who drove opponents nuts when he played a no-holds-barred game for the Boston Bruins in the late 1960s and early 1970s. On the theory that it takes one to know one, Sanderson qualifies as an expert on hated performers.

"A player is disliked because he evokes fear from opponents, be it physical or the fear of embarrassment," said Sanderson, now a Bruins analyst.

Goaltenders usually avoid such notoriety because the very nature of their kamikaze job inspires sympathy rather than infamy. But the New

York Islanders' Bill "My Crease Is A Minefield" Smith changed all that with one swing of his stick at Wayne Gretzky's shins and another at Lindy Ruff's eyes. When Smith showed up in Edmonton for the 1983 Stanley Cup finals against the Oilers, one newspaper featured Billy the Kid's face in the form of a dartboard target on page one.

Compared with goalie Ron Hextall of the Philadelphia Flyers, Smith comes off more like St. Francis of Assisi. Subtlety is not a part of Hextall's constitution, nor is self-restraint. Hextall's list of personal affronts seems as endless as the national highway system and his boiling point around 32 degrees Fahrenheit.

Merely losing an ordinary hockey game — the kind that would have other goaltenders yawning — is apt to send the Brandon, Manitoba native into huge transports of anger. He once broke teammate Sylvain Turgeon's arm in nothing more than a Team Canada workout because of a minor dispute.

In a game against the New Jersey Devils Hextall once viciously clobbered rival goalie Alain Chevrier from behind at game's end for no apparent reason other than the fact that Hextall was the losing goalie. "There was absolutely no reason for him to go after me," says Chevrier, "but that's Hextall."

Devils' defenseman Ken Daneyko has had the urge to blast Hextall right in the kisser. But, then again, who besides the Flyers doesn't get that feeling? "Ron has this knack of getting under your skin," said Daneyko. "He tries to throw you off your game."

A couple of incidents would be enough to place some Filthy McNasties on the bad list but this chap, Hextall, never stops. During the 1987 Stanley Cup finals he pole-axed Kent Nilsson of the Edmonton Oilers with Bunyanesque gusto. The league took such a dim view of the clout that Hextall was suspended for eight games at the start of the following season.

Those who thought Hextall would be deterred by his suspension had another think coming. If anything, he seemed more rambunctious than ever during the 1988–89 season, as Pittsburgh Penguins' (now with Hartford) scoring ace Rob Brown will readily attest. Brown once had the temerity to raise his stick in high glee after flipping a puck past Hextall in the playoffs. "Next thing I knew," Brown recalls, "Hextall was coming after me like I committed a crime or something."

Fortunately for Brown's physical well-being and Hextall's report card, the Penguin conducted an orderly retreat and Ron escaped with neither banishment from the game nor a suspension. It was this brand of behaviour that moved fans throughout the league to chant a derisive "HEX-TALL . . . HEX-TALL" whenever the goalie appeared.

"They hate Ronnie for his meanness," said ex-NHL tough guy John Ferguson, who was the Winnipeg Jets' general manager. "But deep down every fan who boos Hextall wishes he was on *their* team because he's so intimidating."

There's a fine line between positive and negative intimidation.

Hextall crossed that line in game six of the 1989 Wales Conference finals between the Flyers and Montreal Canadiens. Ron's motivation may have been laudable — he claims he was avenging an injury-producing check inflicted on teammate Brian Propp by the Canadiens' Chris Chelios in the opening game of the series. But Hextall's egregiously poor timing astonished even the bully-oriented Flyers' general staff.

Up to that eruption Hextall and the Flyers had played gallantly against the superior Canadiens and in the process had won the hearts of friend and foe alike. Still, Hextall's blood continued boiling over the Chelois–Propp affair. As the clock ticked off the final minutes of the series Ron could contain himself no more. He charged from his crease, tossed his blocker at Chelios, and attempted to maul the Montrealer more in the manner of Hulk Hogan than an all-star goalie. By the time the dust had cleared, the Flyers were eliminated, Hextall was on the NHL carpet again and ultimately spent his summer burdened with the knowledge that he had been socked with a 12-game ouster, the fourth-longest NHL suspension for an on-ice incident.

Flyers officials were outraged by the severity of the sentence — some insiders report that they were privately angry at Hextall — and the goalie was stunned. "What I did," he asserted, "was very regrettable. I deserved a suspension — but 12 games! There would have been no suspension if I wasn't a goalie. You see it all the time, guys going 20 feet to nail a guy and they don't call intent to injure."

Others disagree. Former NHL goalie John Davidson, now a TV analyst, complained, "I have full respect for him as a goalie, but no respect for his tactics. What's it going to be next time — 30 games?"

Controversy followed Hextall right to his South Jersey doorstep the day after he had been handed his suspension. Teams of Philadelphia television crews surrounded his home seeking an interview. His children were at home with a sitter while Hextall attended a figure-skating show at the Spectrum. When he returned home, he was furious upon learning that the crews had disturbed his family and scared his kids. "One guy walked around my house, looking in the windows," he complained. "Another guy rang my doorbell 20 times. My one-year-old kid woke up screaming, scared. My three-year-old was terrified."

Ron himself may not be terrified but now appears penitent over his precarious position vis-à-vis the league. "I realize I can't be suspended anymore," he conceded. "Now I'm under a microscope the rest of my career, so I'd better watch myself."

Whether Hextall can apply the brakes to his runaway temper is a moot question. "His problem," says ex-NHL coach-turned-broadcaster Harry Neale, "is that he's more than careless with his stick. If he were a player who didn't have the protection that goaltenders get, he wouldn't be as hated as he is. But what contributes to Hextall's 'hateability' is that he has that terrific ability to beat you."

Hextall's ability to inspire fear and loathing diminished in 1989–90 and 1990–91 as an unusual series of injuries sidelined him for long periods of time. There have been suggestions among those close to the goalie that the negative reaction he inspired began to affect him.

The hate factor has clearly affected Hextall's family, if not the goalie himself. As far back as 1987, after Ron had won the Conn Smythe Trophy as the most valuable player in the playoffs, his wife, Diane, expressed misgivings to this reporter over the way the public misreads her husband. She was no less vehement on the subject following his 1989 suspension.

"Ron handles the criticism very well," Diane explained. "But it frustrates me, others in the family, and our friends when people who see him play think he's really like that. It couldn't be farther from the truth."

In truth, the off-ice Hextall is far from the hateful rogue depicted by the out-of-town media. For example, a Toronto columnist suggested that he was in need of a psychoanalysis, while a New York reporter described him as plain "rotten." The Ron Hextall his wife knows best is a devoted father to his six-year-old daughter Kristen and four-year-old Bretton. He is intelligent, witty, articulate, and perceptively introspective.

"It may not look it at times," he said, "but I am always in control on the ice. I knew exactly what I was doing when I went after Chelios. I wanted to fight him."

There are more than a few people around the NHL who would at least support Hextall on this point: Chelios deserves a swift kick in the pants if not a punch in the mouth, as Hextall intended to deliver in 1989.

Yet those who know and love Chris Chelios can't understand why so many people dump on the former Norris Trophy winner. And, make no mistake, Chelios was well ensconced on the hate parade long before he knocked Brian Propp unconscious with a from-behind elbow to the head.

"When you've got a player of his size and speed," said Davidson, "he's going to hurt you when he hits you. People hate a player when he hurts others."

How deep the hatred? Consider this: Chelios was well on his way to being named the NHL's best defenseman in 1988–89, yet Wales Conference coach Terry O'Reilly of the Boston Bruins — virulently anti-Chelios — left Chris off the All-Star team. O'Reilly explained that it would be unfair for an alleged cheap-shot artist like Chelios to win the Norris Trophy.

"The fact is," said former NHLer Peter McNab, "that Chelios has been known as someone free with his stick ever since he's been in the league. Some of the more respected people in the league have some pretty severe things to say about him. For example, Chelios's hit against Propp was unnecessary."

Although Chelios has been the centre of several NHL firestorms in his eight-year big-league career, nothing compared with the eruption he triggered in the opening game of the Montreal–Philadelphia 1989 Wales Conference final at Montreal's Forum.

In the second period, the high-scoring Propp lost the puck along the boards. "Chelios," says Neale, "hits from behind."

Nothing better demonstrated the charge than Chelios's move as he approached the Flyer. Propp's helmeted head was facing the protective glass when Chelios swooped in like a dive bomber picking a target. He crushed Propp into the boards, bouncing the forward's head off the glass. Whether the Flyer was unconscious or not at this point is debatable, but this much is certain: he fell back and struck his head on the ice with such force that onlookers feared for his future.

Propp's concussion was not as severe as first feared. He missed one playoff game and then returned to the Philadelphia lineup. Meanwhile, the Flyers screamed bloody murder, claiming that Chelios should have been suspended. As it happened, Chris received neither a game penalty nor league discipline despite a formal protest by the Flyers.

"What Chelios did to Propp," said Hextall, "was far more vicious than what I did to Chelios."

To Chelios's credit, he faced up to an endless number of Flyers' avenger-assaults through the rest of the series and never once turned tail and ran. "He took their best shots," recalled ex-teammate Larry Robinson, "and then put it to Hextall with a big goal in the series-clinching game. Much of the criticism Chris receives is unfair."

Indeed, many Chelios watchers find it hard to comprehend why people like O'Reilly and Hextall rant and rave against their man. When Chelios's 1984 U.S. Olympic hockey coach, Lou Vairo, heard about the anti-Chelios movement in Boston and Philadelphia he thought they were talking about a different Chelios than the one who skated for him.

"I know Chris to be a tough, courageous kid — not a backstabber," said Vairo. "The Propp incident was unfortunate, sure, but how many times do you see the same thing happening like that check into the boards and nobody blinks an eyelash?

"This much I'll grant you, Chris marches to a different drummer. When I had him we'd go at it for weeks on end because he refused to wear socks in his skates. And I'm even talking about in Sarajevo where the cold got *cold*! But he eventually learns his lesson."

In this case the nerves in the tips of his toes were short-circuited so that he *had* to put on a pair of socks.

"Chris doesn't have to stoop to cheap-shot tactics," added Vairo, "because he's such a brave kid. If you were jumped by 20 thugs, he'd be the one guy to come running barehanded to help."

Others argue that Chelios's reputation as a stickman has been well earned and is a prime reason why he is consummately disliked in precincts other than Philadelphia. Like Hextall, Chelios will often execute his foul with a flagrant lack of discretion.

During a game at *le Colisée* in Quebec City, Chris decided that it was time for retribution against Nordiques' needler Paul Gillis. With a bayonet style worthy of the trenches, circa World War I, Chelios planted his stick blade in Gillis's stomach. And if that wasn't horrific enough, the riposte was delivered directly in front of referee Don Koharski!

Spearing is a major no-no in the NHL, worthy of a five-minute major penalty on the spot. "What he did was bad enough," said then Canadiens coach Jean Perron, "but the penalty also put us in a position to lose the game. We were winning 2–1 at the time but there were 19 minutes left in the third period. Fortunately, we won."

Chelios's explanation satisfied both veterinarians and hockey coaches. "It's that pit bull upbringing," he chuckled. "They grow 'em tough in those small European countries [Greece] and I've got this temper that gets me into trouble now and then."

He also has a mouth that has done likewise. A few years ago he nearly incited a Canadiens' dressing-room uprising because of a remark made to then teammate Chris Nilan. Chelios had accused Nilan of telling Mike Lalor — then the team's sixth defenseman — that the five other defensemen had held a meeting to devise a plan to convince Perron to employ only five defensemen. Nilan hotly denied doing anything of the sort and an argument ensued.

In typical Chelios fashion, he played down the uproar. "It was just an argument, the way brothers or sisters have a fight," he explained. "It was a case of someone being there and a little got turned into something bigger."

Now that he is a former Norris Trophy winner, Chelios will be eyed even more carefully and will have to do something about the negative reputation which has followed him since his NHL debut. His onetime college roommate, Mike Blaisdell, recalled that during an exhibition game in the fall of 1986 he and Chelios began tossing punches. It ended when Chris clubbed Mike with Blaisdell's helmet.

Chelios: "It wasn't a class act. I didn't get here for being a fighter or being cheap."

As often is the case with leaders on the hate parade, the off-ice persona is nothing like the boo-inspiring ruffian seen on NHL ponds. Chelios is an excellent example. The man who gave Propp a concussion once was a scrawny kid with braces who wore prescription glasses and played first clarinet in his junior high school band in Chicago.

"I also played piano for a few years," Chelios remembered. "I was musically inclined. My dad wanted me to learn it because he loved listening to the clarinet and the Greek bands. When I was sixteen — with braces on my teeth, and glasses all bent up and broken from hockey — I was 135 pounds. I looked like I was made for something like the clarinet."

Chris's father, Gus, had been in the restaurant and night club business. "Oh, could Chris play the piano," enthused Gus Chelios. "His teacher told me not to stop him from playing because he had long fingers and he was going to be a hell of a piano player. She nearly killed me when I told him he could quit. But he was just way too aggressive to play piano!"

If you believe some of the Montreal tabloids, Chelios also was too aggressive in his off-ice pursuits. Before the 1988 playoffs there was a story about Chelios and teammates Petr Svoboda and Shayne Corson reportedly breaking curfew and getting into a car accident, but Chris countered that it was exaggerated. "He's no worse than any of us were at twenty-four or twenty-five years old," added Canadiens general manager Serge Savard.

Perhaps Chelios's irascibility is best explained by his former University of Wisconsin teammate Gary Suter. "There's that Greek bloodline, you see, so you gotta watch out if you get him mad."

Few players have gotten the enemy madder than Ken "The Rat" Linseman, who has been hated longer than Chelios and Hextall put together even though there is no Greek bloodline to blame.

"He's like having fleas," said Davidson. "You have to get rid of them, but they're always there."

Size — he's a scrawny midget by NHL standards — impelled the centre to live by the sword, so to speak, or he'd die as a hockey player before he ever graduated from junior hockey. In fact, one incident can be isolated as pivotal in moulding the Linseman a-stick-in-time-saves-nine-stitches-in-return image.

He had been skating for the Kingston Canadiens in the Ontario Hockey Association against the Ottawa 67's. Following a whistle, Jeff Geiger of Ottawa charged Linseman and in the ensuing fracas Ken's neck was bent out of shape by a piece of lumber disguised as a hockey stick. Geiger's face looked like a broken bottle of catsup after Linseman kicked him in the face with his skate. A year and a half later Linseman was found guilty of assault by an Ottawa court.

What Linseman didn't know about filthy-dirty play in junior hockey he learned in the World Hockey Association with the Birmingham Bulls. Coached by Glen Sonmor, who as an NHL player would rather fight than switch, the Bulls collectively were the most outrageously ornery team in hockey history. The likes of such wild men as Steve Durbano, Gilles "Bad News" Bilodeau and Dave "Killer" Hanson carried butt-ending, spearing, and high-sticking to an art form. Meanwhile, the skilled Linseman collected points between jabs of his own. "Considering my size," he explained, "it was the way to survival."

When the WHA expired, Linseman was signed by — who else? —

the Broad Street Bullies, and immediately made a favourable impression on Flyers fans. He proved to be an offensive force, but more to the point — as in the end of his stick — Linseman emerged as the NHL quintessential pain in the ass.

Neale, who coached against him, said, "Ken was the ultimate agitator. The average player might take one stab at you but Linseman always took the second stab. He became hateful because he would start a lot of trouble but rarely got into it."

Sanderson: "Linseman has an uncanny ability to aggravate, but if you've got your shit together, you don't care."

During the 1981–82 season Linseman collected 275 penalty minutes and almost as many enemies. "He started out," McNab recalled, "by using his stick to protect himself, but then it got to the point where he began abusing the use of the stick. He was playing for the Flyers and was following the Bobby Clarke mould."

Clarke had captained Philadelphia to a pair of Stanley Cups in 1974 and 1975 and often used his stick like a machete. Linseman not only did likewise but also employed a machine-gun-like tongue as an additional offensive weapon and, if necessary, would put some teeth into his assaults, *real* molars.

In a playoff game against the Nordiques he bit Quebec goalie Dan Bouchard on the finger during a melee around the net. "Now," barked Bouchard, "I know why they call him the Rat."

This was Rat Linseman at his best — taunting Dale Hunter, smirking at Kim Clackson, jabbing his stick in Bouchard's face. He seemed to revel in his role and even had a rat tattooed on his right calf and posed with a rat for a *Hockey News* cover story. In 1984 he reinforced his rodent reputation by sinking his teeth deep enough into defenseman Lee Fogolin's cheek that a doctor was obliged to give Fogolin a tetanus shot.

The Rat's rationale always has been linked to the NHL's broad-and-loose interpretation of the rule book. As long as fighting is tolerated, Linseman figures, what difference does it make *how* he survives? "I've played against a lot of the great ones," said Sanderson, "and what Kenny has done is just what Gordie Howe liked to do — use the stick. Linseman didn't invent it."

While leaving a trail of enemies bent on revenge, Linseman also developed a fair list of former employers who tired of his act. The Flyers dealt him to the Edmonton Oilers, who should have liked him a lot since Ken scored the goal that provided the Gretzkyites with their first Stanley Cup, in 1984. Oilers general manager Glen Sather was so enthused he dealt Linseman to Boston where he performed erratically but well enough, at times, to remain the highest-paid Rat in hockey.

"The thing about Kenny," said former goon Dave Semenko who became an Edmonton broadcaster, "is that you love having him on your side because it's a real pain having him against you. I had it both ways. I know."

The ice rodent NHL players know and loathe so well is approximately 180 degrees removed from Linseman the husband, father, investor, and friend who invariably charms those who deal with him in the non-ice world. "He's very bright, very inquisitive, and very independent," said his agent, Arthur Kaminsky of the New York-based firm Athletes and Artists. "He's certainly not a rat. When my daughter was born, he sent her the nicest present of them all. I guess the bottom line is that my wife, who doesn't like all my clients, likes Ken."

The Bruins soon tired of his act and dispatched Ken to Philadelphia again. Although he had lost some of his bite, the Rat continued to gnaw away at the opposition. When the Flyers again lost interest, Oilers general manager Glen Sather figured he could extract another year or two of quality needling out of cantankerous Ken.

V

THE TOUGH GUYS
SPEAK OUT

Hockey's tough guys rank among the most misunderstood people in sports.

The enforcer — goon, policeman, or whatever — is characterized by the noninformed as some sort of antisocial crazy man who likely would be in jail if he perpetrated in real life some of the assaults committed in the arena. If it were left to an editorial cartoonist, the enforcer would no doubt be depicted as something akin to Conan the Barbarian. Yet the real-life hockey cop is anything but the cretin so often depicted by professional hockey's detractors.

Some of them, such as Montreal's Todd Ewen, are creative off the ice — Ewen is the author of a sensitive children's book — while others, like Islanders defenseman Ken Baumgartner, are articulate and extremely studious. Baumgartner is an A student majoring in political science at Long Island's Hofstra University.

The portrait of the hockey heavyweight as an uncouth loudmouth is thoroughly refuted by Troy Crowder, who speaks softly and would just as soon discuss business or the natural beauty of his native northern Ontario as a hockey fight.

In an effort to better explain what makes these guys tick, a series of interviews was held with them during the 1990–91 season throughout Canada and the United States. The idea was to get the individuals to freely associate as much as possible about themselves, their background, and their business.

As you will see, some were extremely forthcoming while others were guarded in their revelations. Yet it is quite clear that in all cases these rugged individuals take their business seriously, if not defensively.

Chapter 17

CHRIS NILAN

THE ENFORCER WHO WENT TO THE ALL-STAR GAME — ALMOST

Speaks Out

I had interviewed Chris Nilan a few times during his Montreal Cana-diens career but came to appreciate him more as a New York Ranger. Nilan was traded from Montreal to New York on January 27, 1988 as part of a switch of 1989 draft picks. His impact on the Rangers was immediate and positive. The normally boisterous Madison Square Garden fans roared their approval over Nilan's turbulent play and Chris demonstrated that he was an effective offensive threat as well as a ruffian. Our interview took place at the Rangers' suburban Rye, New York training base in October 1989. During our conversation two as-pects of Chris's personality were evident — his whimsical streak and his candour. He did, however, request that one teenage indiscretion be kept off the record although it had made print before. His request was granted.

Nilan's effectiveness as a Ranger was severely curtailed by injury. He was traded to the Bruins on June 28, 1990. As a Bruin, Nilan was welcomed as a conquering hero who returned home. His coach, Mike Milbury, was so enthralled with his play that Milbury invited Nilan to play on the 1991 NHL All-Star team (Wales Conference). The invitation caused an uproar throughout the league. Unfortunately for Nilan he chose to dribble a basketball on Boston Garden's parquet floor a couple of weeks before the All-Star match. The resultant leg injury forced him out of the All-Star lineup.

Chris recovered from the injury sufficiently to rejoin the Bruins for the 1991 Stanley Cup playoffs. As usual, he was a presence, alternately acting as enforcer on Boston's top line with Cam Neely and Craig Janney as well as causing disturbances to disrupt the Hartford Whalers, Montreal Canadiens, and Pittsburgh Penguins.

For Nilan, facing his old Montreal teammates put him in a difficult position. But once he remembered his youth, it was easier for him.

"When I was growing up in Boston," says Nilan, "I hated the Canadiens. Then I got drafted by the Canadiens. I ended up hating the taxes but not the Canadiens."

As a Bruin in the twilight of his career, Nilan played under an old adversary, Mike Milbury. "He hasn't changed any," says Milbury. "I take that back. I think he's more composed than he was at one time in his career."

If Nilan was more composed, it certainly wasn't evident from his penalty numbers. Chris played in just 41 games for Boston in 1990–91, yet led the club with 277 penalty minutes.

"I'll still come to help a teammate," Nilan concludes.

My father got me into skating when I was young. When I was six years old I skated in the city; I skated on a frozen puddle. There was a local guy who had a hockey league for kids around Boston. My father signed me up and I got going in hockey. As far as my aggressiveness on the ice, I would say it was a combination of both my mom (Leslie) and my dad. He was a Green Beret for 33 years. He's jumped out of planes; he's a jungle expert; he's done everything. When I was growing up, he was always on top of me. He didn't let me hang out on the street corners.

My mom would stick up for me at times, but she was pretty firm. My father was a little more reserved at the hockey rink, while my mother was a little more wild.

When I finished four years at Catholic Memorial in Boston, I had to take another year because I didn't do that well in my grades. I had a problem getting into college with my grades, plus I wasn't that sought-after a hockey player. So I went away for a year to Northwood Prep School. I got half a scholarship there and I think it was the best thing to happen to me. I got away from the city, away from my friends, and away from home. There was a big change in my attitude in that one year and I wanted to play pro hockey and wanted to go to college. I ended up going to Northeastern University, coached by ex-Bruin Fernie Flaman.

I have a friend who's a judge in the Boston area. He's a friend of Fernie Flaman. Fernie saw me in Lake Placid and liked what he saw so I got a scholarship to Northeastern. I did a lot better in school. As far as hockey — I got most improved player and ended up not paying for my college.

I got into a fight with a couple of guys and I had to get operated on. I was scared because I had my scholarship. I ended up in the hospital and had an infection in my hand. We had a game that night and

Flaman asked me what happened and I said I was messing around with my mutt and he nicked me on the hand. He came in three days later, and much to my surprise, on the bed it said "human bite." He bagged me. We ended up talking and I told him I was scared to lose my scholarship. He was good to me with that. I didn't want to lie; I hate lying. I wanted to be up front with him but I was scared to lose my scholarship.

I am not a policeman. As for being a *policeman* policeman, I'm not one to say, "If you touch that guy, then I'll get you." I do my thing and I play my game. I just don't concern myself with being a policeman or a goon. If I have to help a teammate, then I will.

I'm fearless to a certain degree, but I'd be a liar if I said I never felt fear. You have to feel it sometimes. I guess I basically have to have an attitude that you don't care, you're not worried about what happens — you just go out and do your job and not think of anything else.

In my first game against the Bruins, I got into fights with Stan Jonathan and Terry O'Reilly. I got a good punch in the nose. It let me know these guys are a little better than the guys down in the minors. I knew O'Reilly was a good fighter but I came in with some good rights, because I knew he was a lefty, but boom, he hit me with a left anyway. I knew I had to establish myself against the Bruins because it was such a rivalry. In my second game I fought "Hound Dog" Kelly [of the Philadelphia Flyers] and I'd say I gave it to him pretty good. My first game was against Atlanta. I get there and all I see is Willie Plett and a ton of big guys. Then we played Philly and they started running around, and I remember Claude Ruel saying, "Yankee boy, you don't have to be scared of anybody out dere — dey are jus' men like us."

Glen Cochrane was the first fight to get me attention. I signed a five-game trial in the minors. I didn't get to play the first four games and then I got to play against Maine and little did I know what players would be there. I more or less went in there fearless. I never fought on the ice but I thought it couldn't be that hard. I knew he was the big guy so I went after him and I cut him open. Then everybody knew who I was and I was fighting every game. I had 304 minutes in 49 games but I also had 25 points, which isn't bad for me.

I think Behn Wilson was tough — Dave Brown, Terry O'Reilly, and Stan Jonathan were about the toughest. Dave Semenko — I think he was bigger than he was tough. I'd have to rank Jay Miller as being one of the toughest — he can throw both hands and take a punch.

The first time I ever talked to Miller off the ice was during the 1989 exhibition season in Cincinnati. He said, "Hi" to me and we started talking about a mutual friend of ours. He just asked about him and then we kept talking, shooting the breeze about how things were going. I asked him how he liked it in L.A., and then [Los Angeles general manager] Rogie Vachon saw him talking to me, and I think he thought he was in trouble.

As he left he said, "Oh, shit, Rogie saw us. I think he's pissed." Needless to say, the first shift on the ice, we ended up fighting. I couldn't believe it, although I kind of sensed it coming. I said to myself, "Holy shit, here we go!" I was ready. I expect that. Just because you know him and talk to him doesn't mean that you can't fight him or play a hard game against the guy. You have to. You're playing for your team and he's playing for his team. I don't have any problems with that.

I won't get tired of fighting like Semenko and Dave Schultz because the reason they got tired was that they didn't play well. Schultz played more than Semenko, who would play then sit on the bench. With me it's more instinctive. It's not that I love to do it, but it's that I know what I have to do. I know when it's time and I'll do it. I really feel I'll do it until the last game I play. I won't let myself get where a coach is going to tell me to fight, because once it happens, there is going to be a confrontation. I wouldn't want anyone telling me to go out and fight. That's when I would feel like grabbing the coach by the tie and throwing him onto the ice.

I've never really had any regrets about a fight because I've never hurt anybody that bad. I've cut guys, broke a nose or two, but I haven't had any regrets about anybody I fought. When it happens, you have to fight to win, you got to fight to get an edge. It's you or the other guy. If I ran a guy and I hit him dirty from behind and hurt him seriously, then I would have regrets. Several years ago, I hit Tomas Jonsson [then of the Islanders]. I had one foot off the ice and I hit him hard. I was worried about him. That's probably the only time in my career that I was worried about someone who I hit hard. I was so happy when he got up and I found out that he was all right. In a fight, no, but when I checked him that night I was scared. I wasn't scared that anyone was going to come after me, because I can deal with that. I was just scared for him.

My wife wasn't too keen on my fighting in the first couple of years because she didn't know all about hockey and I wasn't playing a lot. There'd be times I'd come home and I wasn't happy. I wanted to play but I realized I had to put my time in. She was a little mad at that point, but she's learned to accept it and she'd say she doesn't worry about me when I'm fighting.

Very rarely have I gotten hurt in a fight, [just] a black eye or a bloody nose or my hands were cut and she understands. Hey, I'm making a living. I'm going to put my kids through school and give the best possible life for my family. If it means I have to fight, then I will. This is the route that I chose to follow. I'm going to make the best of it, and get everything I can out of the game before I leave.

At the start of my career I wasn't really pissed off at [Harry] Sinden when I was passed up by the Bruins. I didn't know him and I didn't know what he knew about me. To me it was a surprise just to get drafted [231st overall, fourth last in the draft]. As years went on, I had problems in Boston. There was a lot of bullshit I had to put up with and then Harry Sinden came out and started to be vocal against me. That's what made me say, "Well, he's mad at me?" Why? Because I did what his team did for years in the NHL — kick the shit out of and terrorize other teams? Stan Jonathan, John Wensink, Terry O'Reilly. Who are they kidding? Now because they had a couple of those guys and I threw a little of that shit in their faces they don't like it.

It's like the Middleton thing. [Note: Nilan was suspended eight games in 1985 for butt-ending Rick Middleton, who suffered a broken bridge and two-stitch cut inside his mouth]. I insist to this day that I didn't hit him with the butt end of my stick. He had only two stitches in the back of his mouth, and I hit him with my glove. To this day [October 1989], that's the one black mark against me with Sinden. I'm not one known for taking good hockey players and taking them out of the game. I'll play hard and I'll check them but that's what I have to do.

Ken Linseman has probably aggravated me the most. He's a good team player but a lot of times he gets his stick up and he uses it to protect himself. Sometimes he can get pretty dangerous with the stick around the face. One thing that pisses me off most — and I think it does all players — is guys who come out of the gates ready to rule the world at home, but when they get on the road, they're different players. Like Brian Propp [then of the Philadelphia Flyers, more recently Minnesota North Stars], he plays the game and scores his goals but when he played in Philadelphia he'd use his stick more to slash guys. When he was on the road it was a little different. And maybe Dale Hunter [of the Washington Capitals]. But I have respect for Dale. He plays his game and he'll drop his gloves. But he's always got his stick up. He's a shit-disturber and he does it well. But a guy like Hunter will do it on the road, too, not just at home.

When Paul Baxter was playing in Pittsburgh, he slashed me one time when I was coming up the ice and I slashed him in the back of the leg. He spun around and caught me with the stick and cut me open. I dropped my gloves and went right after him, but he went on the ice and covered up. When we went to the penalty box, I started yelling. I said, "You give me the stick again, and I'll ram it down your throat." I was cut, and I was upset, and he had his helmet off. The refs were giving penalties and I grabbed the puck, stood up, and threw it at him. I hit him in the head; caught him for about ten stitches. They kicked me out of the game.

My father and mother were at that game and my father flipped out afterwards; he was pretty upset. I just said, "Hey, I look at it like, do unto others before they do unto you." Baxter told me he was going to get me, but I figured, give him one first, then he might think otherwise next time. That was the only way I could teach him.

Chapter 18

ALAN MAY

WASHINGTON'S
SECRETARY OF SOCK

Speaks Out

Virtually unknown when he broke into the NHL as a member of the Boston Bruins in 1987–88, Alan May was then dealt to Edmonton where once again he played in only three NHL games in the 1988–89 season. Then he began to see the light at the end of the NHL tunnel when he was traded to the Washington Capitals in 1989.

Where he had once been a virtually useless appendage, May became a regular, first under coach Bryan Murray and then, after Bryan was fired, under his successor, younger brother Terry Murray. May played a total of 77 regular-season games and finished the campaign with 339 penalty minutes. If there was any doubt about who was Washington's enforcer, May's penalty minutes underlined the point.

Alan also managed seven goals and ten assists for 17 points. His spirited play helped Washington to a third-place finish in the Patrick Division and upset playoff victories over the Devils and Rangers in the opening rounds.

For the first time in his professional career, May was held over for a second straight season by an NHL club. General manager David Poile regarded him as a prime asset on the team and in 1990–91 May proved an effective, if not overly productive, member of the team. Ironically, his truculent presence was not enough to satisfy the Caps' felt need for fury. Through the first half of the season the team was outfought enough for one member of the front office to complain, "We've got a team of pussies!" Apparently Poile shared this view and attempted to remedy the problem by dealing for May's chum from his youth hockey days, John Kordic.

May had been well aware of Kordic's turbulent past and attempted to

*ease his entrance to the Caps varsity. But Kordic could not kick his
problem with alcoholism and was suspended for the season.*

*"Of all the Capitals players," says Washington correspondent Mary
McCarthy, "nobody felt more let down by the Kordic incident than
May." McCarthy, who had befriended May early in the season and who
regarded him as an upright individual, taped the following interview
with May.*

I can't remember too well, but my first hockey fight started in a crease.
Actually, I came in and took a shot and the guy pushed me and I pushed
him back and he dropped his gloves and I was really kind of shocked. I
threw so many punches, the guy didn't even come close. All I remember is that his eyes were swollen and I got kicked out of the game.
When I got on the bus after the game the guys were going crazy; they
just thought it was the greatest. I really was fighting more out of fear
then. I didn't know why I dropped my gloves as fast as I did, I just did it
and my hands were going a hundred miles an hour.

I didn't even think of what I was doing. I was just doing it. Maybe
that's why I did so well. The guys on the team loved it and the coach
loved it. He came to talk to me about it and he thought it was great.

I looked up to the big guys because I wasn't that big. I'd look at the
guys who did all the fighting and they usually couldn't skate. I was
little and I could skate pretty well. After a while you get to where you
feel "no one's going to beat me!" It's kind of like Mike Tyson. He got
beaten but he still thinks that no one can beat him.

I was always worried about getting punched in the nose and when it
happened it didn't hurt — or at least not like I imagined. It's no big deal
but I'm sure there are guys out there that can make you feel the punch.

The minor leagues had the same rules against fighting as the NHL,
but you could get away with more down there. You could swing your
stick as much as you wanted and you barely ever got penalized for it.
The refs don't want you to sit in the penalty box the whole game. They
kind of let the games get out of hand.

Some guys got gashes on their face. But you kind of learn how to
survive, really. Someone does something to you and you do it back,
they're probably not going to do it as much. It's not as bad as the movie
Slapshot but it's pretty close.

The Bruins called my house in Edmonton to come and play for them.
I talked to Mike Milbury in the summer. He told me he was going to be
coaching me. He asked if I'd skate in this little camp in Boston so he
could get a look at me. I was under the impression that I was already
going to the camp — the Bruin camp. I was ten minutes into the
scrimmage when he told me, "Don't worry, you'll be coming to camp."
So the rest of the week it was just get in shape and do your own thing.

I did really well in the Boston training camp. I got in some preseason
games, but they sent me down to Maine in the American League

without a contract. I thought, "Another one of these 'good enough to make it but' kind of deals." Mike Milbury made me the captain at the start so I got lots of ice, killed penalties, and played on the power play. He liked that I was willing to fight and stick up for my teammates and worked hard in practice.

I got traded to Edmonton the same year. I led the league with 411 penalty minutes in Maine. I had a chip on my shoulder in the ACHL — if anybody did anything I did something about it. Then I get to the AHL and Mike taught me how to control my aggressions out there. I'd break my stick and try to put someone through the boards every time. I'd just get so out of control. He taught me how to control everything. If someone two-handed you, you picked the right time to force something. I'd skate two extra strides and finish my hit and hopefully the guy would take exception and he'd want to fight to change the momentum of the game. He taught me that hockey is defensive oriented and to get the puck out of your own end.

I've never been rough off the ice. You learn to separate that. It's almost like acting, really. Someone who plays a murderer in a movie is not like that in real life. I kind of enjoyed it sometimes when things were not going well on the ice. Someone was going to pay that night. The first person who pulled the pin out of the grenade got it.

Th first three guys I fought in the NHL were [Gino] Cavallini [St. Louis], Shayne Corson [Montreal], and Ken Daneyko [New Jersey]. They all got the instigator penalty, which was good for me. I played well, too, before I went back to the American League.

I barely ever use my mouth to get a response. There are certain guys who do react to it and take bad penalties. So you use it on those kinds of guys. I keep my mouth shut and the referees appreciate it.

To win a fight, you have to be prepared and composed while you do it. If you're out of control, you might win big but you also might lose big. The teams that do the best are the teams where the fighters don't lose a lot of fights. If you're winning 4–2 for instance, and you go out and the other guy takes you to the cleaners, your team is probably going to lose the game because the momentum shifts. You can't take bad penalties and waste fights. When it's 10–1, you don't go out at the end of the game and fight. You want to get a rapport with the referees; you don't want to upset them. You have to calculate everything you do. That means turn the other cheek whether you think you can handle the guy easily or not. You have your work cut out for you with some guys trying to stay away. When you're on a good, smart team like the 1989–90 Capitals, they support everything you do as far as physical play. They figure that if we had to turn the other way there had to be a reason for it. They would pat you on the back just as much for not doing it as they would when you did it a lot.

There are a lot of coaches who send guys out just to fight. You know that if a guy hasn't played a whole game and suddenly he's out there, I don't have to be a rocket scientist to know what to do. No coach has ever had to tell me to go out there to fight, I just did it. I've done it so many times that I think I know the right time to do it, and sometimes when it's tied 2–2 in the third period it has to be done. As long as there are rules for it, you can know how to get around it.

Sometimes I look at fighting and think it's disgusting and dumb. Earlier in the year there was a team that came in and we were beating them soundly and all they were doing was swinging their sticks as hard as they could and we ended up with four guys hurt. There was nobody on our team who was prepared to fight. I don't like it done that way. I kind of like it when two guys square off. I like going in the corner chasing a puck and one guy hits the other a little harder than the other guy likes and they get at it. That's fine. But I don't like when one team sends five guys out to gang up. I don't like the cheap stick swinger or the high cross-checks or hitting from behind.

Fighting does help to police the stick stuff. If there was no fighting and someone were to break his stick on me I'd probably use my stick or give one punch. One punch done cheaply can do more damage than a fair fight. You can knock a guy out for a year, like Joe Kocur did to Brad Dalgarno a couple of years ago.

I'm just trying to win and get the momentum. You want to get their team down. If you're playing at Madison Square Garden and the fans are cheering and I go in and win a fight real good I take the momentum because they are no longer cheering; they're down a few levels.

You're just trying to land your punches. Everybody gets hurt most of the time when they fall off their skates. Throwing a lot of punches doesn't mean you're going to land them. The percentages of landing a punch aren't very good.

Chapter 19

BASIL McRAE

DON'T CALL ME GOON, PLEASE

Speaks Out

When Basil McRae was interviewed by correspondent Michelle Dye, he was a reluctant subject. He didn't fancy himself a goon and was loath to discuss the vicious side of the game. But McRae, who was team captain, has had a vital role with the North Stars, and since he was otherwise gracious about the interview, his thoughts were considered worthy of use.

As enforcers go, McRae has proven himself a survivor. He is a ten-year man in the NHL, with stints in Quebec, Toronto, Detroit, and most recently Minnesota. Basil's most productive season was 1988–89 when he tallied 12 goals and 19 assists for 31 points. His penalty total was 365 minutes. A year later, though sidelined with injuries that trimmed 14 games off his playing time, McRae led the league in penalties with 351 minutes.

Basil's importance to the North Stars was evident with his appointment as team captain. Another point of McRae's value was evident by his salary. While forwards were scoring twice or even more than thrice his totals, McRae was way ahead of them on the salary scale. McRae's annual paycheque in 1990–91 came to $230,000.

Whether or not he's worth it is a moot point. Perhaps Basil was more conspicuous by his absence during the 1990–91 campaign. An injury sidelined him for the first half of the season. When he returned, the North Stars were mired in the slough of despond. Many of the players realized that they were destined to be traded to the expansion San Jose Sharks the following year and did not feel a true part of the club. Compounding problems was the fact that abysmally low attendance had hurt club morale despite the vigour of new owner Norman Green.

For a time at midseason a number of critics opined that the North Stars would finish last in the Norris Division and miss the playoffs. The team's turnabout was directly traced to the return of McRae to the line-up. By early March, Minnesota boasted one of the best records in the month since the All-Star game had been played in Chicago. McRae's contribution both in the dressing room and on the ice was unmistakably upbeat. When the dust had cleared at season's end, the North Stars had made the playoffs for the third straight season, all with McRae in the lineup.

Basil then played a major role in one of the most extraordinary playoff sagas in NHL annals, as his North Stars overcame Chicago, St. Louis, and Edmonton to reach the Stanley Cup finals. McRae teamed with tough guy Shane Churla, but instead of playing the role of mindless goons, the pair played effective rough hockey while suckering opponents like the Blackhawks, Blues, and Oilers into irrational penalties. Minnesota's power play exploited the opponents, enabling McRae's underdog team to meet Pittsburgh in the finals.

North Stars coach Bob Gainey unfailingly inserted McRae in crucial situations and the captain responded nobly. Here we had another case of a goon turned effective hockey player. What made the saga even more heart-warming was the fact that he was doing it with one of the rare Cinderella teams of sport.

I'm definitely a role player. I think every player in the NHL has a certain role that he excels in. I look at myself as a good, tough winger that's going to go up and down my wing and not hurt the team defensively. I know that I've gotta hit and cause a lot of commotion when I'm out there. I just have to play good, tough hockey and be driven to that. I have to be tough on the puck and really be hitting. As far as the fighting part, I don't think that's anybody's role. It's just something that happens and it's how your temperament is. I find myself in that position more because of my temperament; probably because I hit more and try to get more involved and play more aggressive hockey.

I've never had a coach that's really come right out, tapped me on the shoulder and said to me, "Go get him." There's been situations where coaches get upset and they see what's happening on the ice and they get pretty ticked off about it but it's more of a general phrase of "Somebody get that guy" or whatever. A lot of times, I'll take it upon myself to be that guy. If it gets the team fired up, I'll do it.

I think I've always realized my limitations as far as my skill level goes. I knew what type of player I had to be. I wasn't going to be a guy that was going to go end-to-end or anything like that. I always wanted to improve myself and my skills that I had. I always played left wing, so I watched other left wingers in particular and where I thought I was weak, I'd watch the guys who were good. Like if I was weak at taking the puck off the boards, I'd watch guys who were good at taking the puck off the boards. And of course you watch the guys who score a lot, and see how you could score better. But I never really patterned myself after one certain player.

I know my first fight took place at a young level. They kept happening. A lot of them actually weren't very good experiences because I was born in a small town and I always played a level ahead, so a lot of times I was on the wrong end of it.

My first NHL fight was in St. Louis. It was against a guy I played against in junior so I wasn't overly nervous. I don't want to mention any names. The first few fights I was nervous because I watched these guys on television and I thought they were a little tougher than they really were.

For me, winning 20 fights isn't a successful year. To have a successful year is for me to score 20 goals.

I don't really think about fighting before the game. I know it's probable, or there's a good chance it's gonna happen. I don't go around telling everyone who I beat up because I've probably lost more than I've won [laughs].

I've never fought off the ice — as far as in the hallway or in the parking lot. There've been times where I thought maybe it would happen. Sometimes, there's certain guys that if you see them off the ice, you're pretty uncomfortable. You never know what might happen but you try to avoid that because you know it's not good for the game. I try to leave it behind me. I don't want the public to say, "Well look at this guy, he's just a hoodlum, he'll give hockey a bad name."

Fighting is kind of spontaneous, but you know who you're fighting. A lot of times you play with certain guys and don't want to fight them, or if it does happen you just kind of laugh it off afterwards. I guess one guy I won't fight is my brother when I play against him. But everybody else is open game, I guess. Of course there are a couple of guys like Bob Probert [laughs] that you really don't want to fight; but you might be in that situation. If you're going to play aggressively, you're going to fight quite a bit. I try to make it my policy that maybe sometimes I don't want to — but I always will.

I'm not out to take a cheap shot. I want to hit hard and clean, play tough, but that's with the guys who are going to play that way. If I ever fought a guy like Gretzky, they'd have 20 guys coming after me and probably ten of them would be on my own team.

I don't think it's good to change your image, because you've gotta do what brought you here unless you've developed into a good player — like Rick Tocchet, who came in and fought and played aggressively. There are times you have to do what's best for the team. Whether it's a guy like Tocchet, who scores 50 goals, or a guy like me who scored nine or ten, there are times when I have to avoid a fight. If we're ahead 4–3 or I'm on the checking line, I don't want to take a bad penalty. You've got to be smart about it. If it's something that's unavoidable, that's tough. You've got to pick your spot sometimes. Everyone in hockey has been in that situation where a fight isn't the best thing for the team or it isn't the best thing for yourself — like being on a roll in the game and you want to keep things going.

I don't ever want to be in a position where I'm really scared, but I know if I'm not nervous before a game or a fight then I'm not ready. It's a fine line between being nervous and scared. I've learned over the years that I'm thinking about the team all game and I know what I want to do to prepare myself. I think you can psyche yourself out if you're going to sit there and worry about another player. There's no sense getting yourself uptight and taking away from all the other aspects of the game when you're worried about fighting some guy. If it happens, it happens. You've gotta let human nature take its course out there.

I don't think there's any secret to good fighting. Every guy that fights has won and lost a fight. A lot of it is balance. It's not like boxing. A fight in hockey is not premeditated. It's not like I strategically figure out how I'm going to beat a guy.

Last year I tried Velcro sleeves. I guess after being washed a few times, they had gotten a bit looser. They said not to do it anymore and I didn't want to do anything illegal. It wasn't a gimmick and it wasn't for attention.

The only thing that upsets me about referees in the NHL is that if I get into a fight with a guy like Joey Kocur we both get five minutes. But if a guy who doesn't fight as much instigates a fight with me, there's a good chance that I'm going to get a two-minute instigator [penalty] whether I instigated or not. I think a lot of times the referees have already determined who starts a fight, and it's not necessarily true. They have to realize that there are antagonistic people in the NHL. They're more an instigator than the guy who finishes a fight. Some referees are a little insecure that the game might get out of hand and so they have a tendency that if two guys fight they'll give them five and ten, which kind of ticks you off a bit because you're sitting in the box for 15 minutes and it takes away from your game or from the flow and you miss the whole period. It's tough; they've got a job to do and they're trying to keep the game in control but a lot of times they should let two guys fight, bang, get it over with, give them each five and let's get on with the hockey game.

My family doesn't say much about fighting. It's my job, it's my life. They're supportive. They're kind of aggressive people themselves so it's not like "Oh." My wife in particular; she doesn't really get upset about it at all. She knows a lot of times it's going to happen. She knows that when I come home with a black eye or stitches or whatever, that it's part of the game. I don't bring it home and that's probably the main reason why it's not a problem at home. I don't sit there and talk about the fight I had or anything. I'll sit there and talk all night about how I should've scored a goal or maybe I let a check go and someone scored because of me.

As a player, I've been fortunate enough to play for a few years and I've had a chance in the NHL to play many roles — not to just go out and fight. I've had a chance to play on a defensive line and play with some good players. I know I won't be remembered as a great hockey player, but I just want to probably be known as a guy who won something and came to work every day.

Chapter 20

THE ENFORCERS AND THE RANGERS' QUEST FOR THE STANLEY CUP

TROY MALLETTE

TOO GOOD TO BE TOUGH

Speaks Out

At the start of the 1990–91 season tall Troy Mallette was viewed as one of the NHL's top enforcers. He had established a reputation for testy play a year earlier, especially because of a cross-check he delivered during the 1990 playoffs that hospitalized Islanders defenseman Jeff Norton. Mallette was interviewed early in the 1990–91 season by correspondent Tracy Pattison. Pattison found him to be very friendly, articulate, and animated.

Open and talkative, Mallette saw his role change as the season unfolded. The insertion of Tie Domi in the lineup and, later, Joe Kocur, enabled coach Roger Neilson to focus Mallette on his offensive and checking roles, thereby diminishing his need to be an enforcer.

As a kid I was pretty quiet. I was more of a goal scorer than anything else. Back in Levack [his hometown in Ontario], I used to have five- or six-goal games and seven or eight points. It was great, but that was when I was younger.

When you break into the league you've gotta prove to your team-mates and to other teams that you're not going to be pushed around. I was put into a position in 1989–90 where I had to protect guys a little bit because our enforcer, Chris Nilan, was hurt.

That opened the doors. You have to do it in your first year, as far as I'm concerned, regardless of whether you're a goal scorer or whatever. You've gotta show that you're not gonna be pushed around, whether it's pushing and shoving back, or fighting back.

So I was killing two birds with one stone — getting it out of the way. And penalty minutes just piled up. I wasn't planning on getting that many and I don't think I'd be able to do it again. It's just something that happened.

In 1989–90, I was playing on the power play and the chances were there but I didn't have the confidence. I'd just get the puck and I'd shoot it right away without looking and picking a corner. In 1990–91 I had a little bit more confidence to take a little bit of time to shoot. I'm going to flow and take advantage of as many chances as I can in scoring goals.

I hope I'm not fighting as much in the future but if I do, I do. That's nothing I'm gonna worry about. If I have to do that for my career I'll do it, but I'd like to become a complete player where I can do almost anything — not be a star at everything but hopefully be able to do everything well enough to be able to play in all situations.

It is hard for me to picture being a Rick Tocchet right now. He's an all-star, he gets played on the power play, penalty killing, and every third shift. He gets so much time to produce and you have to be given the chance to do that. Hopefully, in the next couple of years I'll have the opportunity, but you know, it's all stuff you have to build up to be able to put in those circumstances and hopefully, in time, that'll come.

In my first year of junior, I was sixteen years old and we had a team that wasn't really too tough so I was put in a position where I had to protect myself because no one else was going to do anything like that because they weren't like that. They had a hard time protecting themselves, let alone me. So I was put in a spot when I was sixteen to defend myself, and out of the first ten games I ended up fighting three of the tougher guys in the league and they all worked well. I didn't get real beat up and I held my own and I kind of got a little bit of a name for myself in the league, as well as for my teammates, which was really good. I realized that that's what you have to do when you're in there for your first year.

A lot of times when you get in a fight and you're down, say 2–1 or 3–2, maybe something like pumping your fists in the air after a fight gets them going. It doesn't do that much for me, but maybe the team, and the fans, are in it now. I think it's a positive effect for everybody on the team. I try not to do it too often because I kind of feel stupid. Maybe it's okay doing it at the time, but when I look later on TV and I see it, I say, "Oh geez, what an idiot!" But what can you do?

Every game is a new game. Every tough guy on every team is someone you have to tell yourself, "You know what he's gonna do tonight? Better watch your back." I don't go to bed thinking that I have to play Troy Crowder tomorrow, or Ken Daneyko or Mick Vukota. It's no big deal; it's just a game. If I have to fight, I have to fight. It's nothing I lose any sleep over.

I agree with Wayne Gretzky about banning fighting. I'd just as soon go out and check as hard as I can every game and not drop the mitts. That's no problem. But frustration can set in. I once got in a fight with

Alan May of Washington. There were six minutes left and I hit some-one in the boards. I didn't think it was a penalty. We were losing 6–3 and the ref gives me a penalty. I'm frustrated and bitter. I'm going to the box and he's standing there and he's the guy that knocked my tooth out last year. So I said sooner or later I'll get a chance to get him back. I said, "Well, this is just as good a time as ever. I'm mad." So it just happened.

Frustration is one of the biggest reasons they still allow fighting. Of course there are guys who sit on the bench for two periods. Then they come off the bench and go at someone and grab them by the shirt. That's simply a case of just going out there to fight. That's wrong. I don't go for that. I can honestly say I've never done that. Even when I hit someone cleanly he's going to get mad and I've gotta defend myself. In other cases, they hit me, I'm pissed off, so I fight them.

Sometimes when you get in a scuffle you just lose all senses; nothing really matters; you don't care what you do or how you do it. You can get in trouble that way or you can look stupid.

A fight is over at different times with different people. Alan May and I have this understanding. In one game, I ended up landing on top of him and he said, "Aw, that was a cheap one," and it *was* a cheap one, I'll admit it. But I was on top and his face was right there and I had about six inches to keep hitting but I knew it was a cheap hit and I shouldn't be doing any of this, so I just stopped and said, "Okay, I'm off, don't worry," and I got off. In other cases, where someone jumps me from behind or starts a fight with me and I'm not ready and I have the opportunity to give him the last cheap shots, I'm gonna do it because I'm pissed. You want to make sure he doesn't jump you again.

As long as I don't kill or paralyze anyone, I don't feel bad about what I do. As mad as I might be at someone, I'd never want to paralyze anyone or anything like that. That's my worst fear. But, as far as knocking out teeth, breaking noses, if it happens, it's part of the game.

You can't get scared. Maybe after a game you say, "Oh geez, I could've been hurt." You can't worry about it. Things like that happen.

JOE KOCUR

THE INVISIBLE GOON

Speaks Out

Rarely in NHL annals has a team more blatantly employed a goon for what it purports to be winning hockey than the Rangers in March 1991 when general manager Neil Smith acquired Joey Kocur from the Red Wings.

To say that Kocur had suffered from a checkered past would be roughly equivalent to suggesting that Al Capone had an occasional brush with the law. As a Red Wing Joey's off-ice problems often were as harsh as his on-ice behaviour. In one episode, he was charged with attacking a waitress in Boston.

Kocur's notoriety stemmed directly from his fists. Along with the equally turbulent Bob Probert, Kocur gave the Red Wings a mean-spirited one-two punch on the forward wall. Kocur's right cross and uppercut became the scourge of the league, and on at least one occasion he literally punched a player right out of the league.

In a game against the New York Islanders at Nassau Coliseum late in the 1988–89 season, Islanders forward Brad Dalgarno checked a Red Wing heavily into the boards. Shortly thereafter, Kocur began stalking Dalgarno until he finally suckered the Islander into a fight. One of Kocur's punches sent Dalgarno reeling — right into the hospital.

Dalgarno was finished for the season with a broken cheekbone, quit hockey for a year, and returned again in 1990–91. By that time, Kocur's evil reputation had peaked, although his on-ice performance had markedly slipped. Under new Detroit coach Bryan Murray, he scored little and assisted less. Inevitably, he became the subject of trade rumours.

While this was going on, the New York Rangers were dominating the Patrick Division and were regarded as one of the more likely contenders for their first Stanley Cup in 51 years. Despite the Rangers' obvious success, two influential New York area reporters, Mark Everson of the New York Post and Walt MacPeek of the Newark Star-Ledger, insisted that the team was not tough enough and required an enforcer. Obviously, general manager Neil Smith was swayed to that viewpoint. Less than an hour before the trade deadline on March 5, 1991, Smith dispatched gifted forward Kevin Miller along with defenseman Dennis Vial and rugged collegian Jim Cummings to the Red Wings for Kocur and Swedish defenseman Per Djoos.

The deal was greeted with enthusiasm in some quarters and criticized as an idiotic move in others.

Smith's contention was that Kocur's presence would eliminate inhibitions suffered by the smaller but talented Rangers. He called Kocur's acquisition "the final piece of the Rangers playoff puzzle."

The pro-Kocur media, led by Everson and MacPeek, immediately jumped on the bandwagon endorsing the deal.

Yet a nucleus of vocal and significant critics could be heard. None was more angry than New York Times columnist Dave Anderson. A Pulitzer Prize winner and one-time hockey writer with the New York Journal-American, Anderson was not a dilettante when it came to the ice game. But he was quick to admit that he had become discouraged by gratuitous fighting and was severely critical of the Kocur trade in his widely read column titled "Rangers Rent a Goon."

Smith was understandably defensive about the criticism. "Joey is more than a goon," countered Smith. "He's a hockey player as well."

Just how much of a hockey player was debatable. In Kocur's debut *against the Nordiques, in Quebec City, he was singularly unproductive as the Rangers were humbled by the last-place Nordiques. Kocur also failed in the physical department. Felled by a thunderous check delivered by Quebec defenseman Randy Velischek, Kocur left the ice and was hospitalized with a punctured lung. He missed the ensuing game against the Islanders, returning to the Rangers' lineup against the Chicago Blackhawks.*

Kocur's productivity remained nil but his penchant for controversy stayed at its disturbingly high level. Against the Blackhawks at Chicago Stadium on March 10, Kocur hit Blackhawks goaltender Ed Belfour with his stick and was suspended for four games by NHL vice-president Brian O'Neill. Since the league allows a team a grace period to appeal — it was not an automatic suspension — before launching a suspension, Kocur was allowed to play in four more games. In the match immediately following his hearing, Kocur had an opportunity to display his physical assets. New York was playing its arch rival from across the Hudson River, the New Jersey Devils. In a game that opened with relentless hitting, Kocur did little to intimidate the Devils except occasionally grimacing at aging Soviet defenseman Slava Fetisov. Kocur took an unsportsmanlike conduct penalty in the first period with Brendan Shanahan, and a morale-hurting slashing penalty in the third period that effectively stifled any Ranger comeback attempt.

What had been billed as a major heavyweight matchup between Kocur and the Devils champ Troy Crowder never materialized. In the first period Crowder checked Kocur heavily into the boards, away from the puck which had been cleared out of the zone. Crowder shoved his hand at Kocur to free himself for retaliation. Only when the Devils' large right wing skated away did Kocur respond, stick-checking Crowder from behind. When Crowder began to turn to face Kocur, the Ranger tied him up and held on until the officials arrived.

Kocur's obvious ineffectiveness was pervasive throughout the game. When the Rangers still had an opportunity for a comeback in the third period, Kocur took the inane penalty that effectively halted any Ranger hopes for a victory. The Rangers lost 5–2, marking their eighth consecutive loss since acquiring Kocur.

Ranger fans who normally would be enthused about the addition of a goon were rapidly becoming disenchanted with the Kocur era. They would get another view of Pal Joey on March 17 against the Pittsburgh Penguins, who had moved to only one point from the New Yorkers in the race for first place in the Patrick Division. Instead of helping the Broadway Blueshirts, Kocur was his own — and his team's — worst enemy.

In the second period, with the score tied 2–2, Kocur speared Pittsburgh defenseman Ulf Samuelsson in the groin and then, as the New York Times pointed out with revulsion, "stood over him like a victorious gladiator" and threw away his broken stick. Kocur was immediately assessed a major penalty, during which Pittsburgh scored the game-winning goal. As a result of the loss, the Rangers dropped out of first place and kindled a firestorm of criticism regarding Kocur.

Compounding the felony was the fact that the spearing penalty was his fourth major stick-related infraction of the season, so without a hearing, he was automatically suspended for three games starting with the Rangers' next game at Pittsburgh. Thus the goon-saviour was, in effect, removed from the Ranger lineup for the final two weeks of the home stretch.

Not surprisingly, Rangers general manager Neil Smith had to crank up his alibi machine into high gear. "It's been a rotten bit of luck on our part," Smith said. "The guy is playing well but somebody goes down, he gets a penalty. If someone else was in the same situation nothing would have been called."

Others who saw the spear thought otherwise, including Rangers radio colour commentator Sal Messina, who succinctly said, "There is no doubt that was the right call and it deserves five minutes."

Smith, of course, was blowing smoke to conceal what appeared to be a major blunder. When he obtained the enforcer he knew that Kocur had long been a marked man and that referees would be eyeing him more than they would a cleaner player.

Joey himself seemed stunned by his misfortune. Newsday columnist Joe Gergen summed up prevailing opinion when he wrote, "You couldn't blame his teammates if they started calling him Joe Bftsplk, the character from Li'l Abner comic strip who was followed by a black cloud wherever he went."

As for Kocur, he had no choice but to wait out the schedule in the hopes of helping the Rangers in their playoff drive. "There are always times when things go bad," he said, "but not on a scale like this. It's just been setback after setback, and with the team not winning, it's been magnified. Whenever I feel I'm getting going, I get my legs cut out from under me."

In the opening playoff round against Washington, the Rangers were upset in six games. Rather than being "the final piece" in the Rangers' Stanley Cup puzzle, Kocur was conspicuous only because of his inconspicuousness.

Kocur was interviewed by reporter Ashley Scharge at the Rangers' training and practice rink in Rye, New York during the first round of the Stanley Cup playoffs. The following are Kocur's observations about his hockey growth and career.

The first time I can remember putting on a pair of skates was behind our house up on the farm, in Kelvington, Saskatchewan. You could call it a pond. Actually, it was a pasture where the animals were kept. I remember going up there and we had to keep our boots on to clean some of the snow off the ice. Then we could put our skates on.

My first hero was Bobby Orr. I always wanted his number and to be able to play like him. But when I got older, people that I idolized and wanted to play like were Terry O'Reilly and Al Secord. I was a defenseman in minor hockey and Orr was a rushing defenseman. I wanted to be a rushing defenseman. He was great and he was the man every kid dreamed to be like.

I was a tough player in junior but when I started out I wasn't so tough. I just went up and down my wing and played a basic style. The coach at the time, Gerry James, who had been a great Canadian Football League player and also played NHL hockey for the Maple Leafs, pulled me over one day after practice — probably 20 games into the season — and told me if I wanted to make a name for myself and get recognized or possibly make a hockey career, I would have to get an identity, have something people want to see. He didn't come out and tell me to fight, but he knew and I knew what I could do best and that would be a tough player from that point on.

I was excited. I had a purpose now. When I first got there, I was young and real naive, just coming off the farm and I didn't know what to do. But he gave me a purpose right then and there for the year and as it turned out that purpose was for a career.

The first guy I fought in junior was Leroy Gorski. I remember he called me on. I had never fought before and that was pretty much it and we dropped the gloves. I asked him how he felt. He knew I was probably scared and took me in pretty good. He showed me how to do it, that's for sure — and he showed me how to take a punch. I learned right then and there he wasn't very big but he was tough. Funny thing was that when I played in Saskatoon a couple of years later, he was my roommate. It was my first fight and he beat me pretty good.

When I played with Saskatoon he was a small guy. He was mentally tough. Nobody intimidated him. He'd go up to the biggest guy on the other team and do what he had to do. It showed me size isn't the difference. I guess it's not the size of dog and fight, but the size of fight and dog.

I don't remember my first fight in the NHL but I can remember an early fight. We were in Minnesota. I had been called up a short time before. I ran into Dave Richter at centre ice and I knew he wanted to fight because he was a tough guy and wanted to fight and he was big. He dropped his gloves and I couldn't get mine off because we were in tight so I grabbed his right hand and left my glove on because I didn't want him to hit me. I didn't know he was a lefty and he started throwing lefts. By the time I got my gloves off, he was probably tired out and had nothing left after that.

I don't know how to explain how different media personalities categorize fighters — or goaltenders or scorers. Between players, we don't talk about it much. I guess through some of the fights I had or things that happen, important people have picked up the paper or seen the fight on TV and come to the conclusion that I'm a good right-hand man. I never thought of myself as that but if they said that, then it's fine.

My role with the Rangers is going to be the same wherever I play — I've got to be an enforcer. If that means pick fights or cause fights, then I will. My role will be to protect guys like Bernie Nicholls and Darren Turcotte — the guys who are going to get the goals to win the games; the guys who are hopefully going to bring us the Stanley Cup. I'm not going to win the Stanley Cup. I'm just going to protect those players who have capability.

An enforcer is someone who is there to stick up for his teammates. I would call someone a goon who goes out to fight. An enforcer is someone there to stick up for the smaller guys or stick up for his team or one that fights for the team to get the team going or protect the team. The other one — the goon — goes out and just fights.

When I was playing junior hockey that's when I watched the Secords and O'Reillys or looked at the newspapers and read the penalty stats. They weren't goons by any means but they would go out there and play their shifts and if something happened, they did something about it. They were good hockey players; they did more than fight. You look at any one of those guys on those hockey teams and they [the players] think the world of them — as hockey players and as people. That's what I saw in them and wanted to be like.

I feel like I'm starting to be like that. When I was in my last few years with Detroit, I wasn't getting sent out to fight; I was getting sent out to be a player and to play the game. I wasn't a liability on the ice and that's something I want to make sure it stays that way. But if someday my hand gets bad or fighting penalties are stricter, I still want to be able to play the game.

My coach in Detroit, Jacques Demers, was a real motivator. He knew how to get the players ready. I guess that that was his strong point. He gave me a chance to play and always told me where I stood.

With my tough Detroit teammate Bob Probert it wasn't like you cover my back and I'll cover yours type of thing. Maybe if he got in a fight with someone and hurt himself, then when I got out there, or vice versa, we always covered for each other.

Like with the Brad Dalgarno incident. He ran one of our players pretty badly early in the game and I just went out to stick up for that player. I remember that shift. He was taunting me all shift. I guess he was making me more pissed off. We were in pretty close and when I hit him, I didn't know I hurt him like that. I just hit him with a punch and I read in the paper the next day that I hurt him pretty seriously. I can't let that type of thing bother me. It's part of the game and part of my job. Things like that happen in a fight.

My most memorable moment came in the 1987 playoffs — the first year Jacques Demers was coaching in Detroit. We had home ice advantage. We were down to the Leafs three games to one and we had a big meeting and all that. We came back and Jacques told me he was going to put me on Wendel Clark as a checker because Wendel and I were good friends and neighbours in Kelvington. He was their team and was the main reason they were winning. I just started checking him and our team started to get a little confidence. They changed goalies and Glen Hanlon was great in goal. The next three games were six days of what every athlete dreams of. When we beat them 3–0 in the final game, the fans went crazy.

I'm sure it's a lot easier coming to the rink without bruises or cuts all over your hand. Those things aren't much fun because it makes it tough to practice. As for fighting, it's always going to be there, it's always part of the game and I enjoy it.

TIE DOMI

CLOWN OR COMPETITOR?

Speaks Out

After being dealt from Toronto to the Rangers in the summer of 1990, the fighting fireplug, Tie Domi, had instant impact on the Rangers, although his value was as debatable as his size. The Ranger media guide lists Domi as 5'10" but in person he appears no taller than 5'8", which would make him one of the most belligerent little guys in NHL history, reminiscent of the Bruins' Stan Jonathan, a Tasmanian Devil on ice who played in the late 1970s. There is no disputing Domi's effervescence. He radiates good humour between bouts and — this is a sad commentary on the New York hockey media — last year obtained more ink than Rangers leading scorer, Mike Gartner.

Unlike other subjects interviewed on hockey violence, Domi had neither compunctions nor restraint in addressing his functions as an enforcer. Correspondent Tracy Pattison interviewed him at the Rangers' Rye, New York, Playland practice rink in Westchester County following a workout. Domi was open to questions and candid in his replies. Like so many of his colleagues, he was defensive about the importance of being an enforcer. Throughout the interview Domi exuded pride in his profession and delight that he was being featured in a work on hockey cops.

As a postscript it should be noted that Domi agreed to the interview just a week and a half after the death of his father, whom he held in the highest esteem.

I developed in juniors. My first year I was just a tough guy, didn't score many goals or anything. My second year, I had one goal up to

Christmas, I think, and I had 250 penalty minutes, and then I got 22 goals after Christmas. That's when I improved as a hockey player. I was just getting the space, the room from being a tough guy and nobody really wanted to hit me. So I got room in front of the net to score goals. I was drafted in the second round, 27th overall in the NHL.

I like to be myself, I like to be Tie Domi. People compare me to Stan Jonathan, formerly of the Boston Bruins. I never saw him play but it's an honour to be compared to the guy. People also compare me to Tiger Williams. Until I achieve what those guys achieved in the NHL and become a proven player like they were, then I don't really want to be compared to them.

Off the ice I'm pretty shy and quiet. I'm still shy when I don't know a person. I get along with everybody. I get along with all of my teammates and friends.

When I was in the OHL, I was known as the toughest guy in the league for the last two years that I played. I always fought bigger guys, and I beat all of them. That's why they called me the toughest guy.

I knew I didn't have the talent that a Guy Lafleur has or anything like that. I always scored goals but I was an aggressive player and I liked to hit and that's how I think it all started. When I got to Junior C I was so small and I would be hitting everybody and I would score too, but I would hit everybody and the older guys in the league would get mad at me and they would end up dropping the gloves and that's how I would fight. I wouldn't say I won every fight but I think that's where all the fighting started, and right from there I fought in Junior B and A and led the leagues in penalty minutes. People must think I'm pretty deceiving looking because I'm so small and they think, "Hey, this guy's not going to hit me" and right away they drop their gloves, so I drop my gloves. I'll never back down from anybody; that's one thing I'm grateful to my father for; he gave me heart and it's a big heart.

My first fight in Junior A was against a guy named Bryan Marchment, who came to the NHL with Winnipeg. The fight was in the first 28 seconds of the game. I got kicked out because I wanted to prove myself against him. I went after him and fought him, so I got kicked out.

Kris King has been a big influence on me. He was a proven player. In his fourth year of junior, I watched how he played and I tried to play like he did and when I didn't, I'd watch every time he was on the ice. I was fortunate to play in Peterborough. The coach there, Dick Todd, never told me once to fight. When I tell people that they just laugh. He was like my father in junior hockey. I still respect the guy and if it weren't for him, I don't think I'd be playing anywhere.

Playing in the Toronto organization later on was a learning experience. I got sent down to Newmarket [American Hockey League] and it seemed like I got lost in the shuffle. I wasn't really getting the opportunity to play even in the minors. When I got called up, I only got called up for the Detroit games and I knew I was just getting called up for those games.

I got so much media there for being a tough guy, with headlines like "Domi's going to be fighting this or Domi's going to be fighting that" and it really bothered me a lot. That's one thing that changed in New York; they really don't blow you up to be a fighter. The media kind of gives you a chance to get a reputation for yourself; they never blow things out of proportion.

My role is as a sparkplug. A lot of guys here called me Sparkplug or Sparky. I try to get the team going if the team is down, and even when we're not down and we just need some hits. Roger really stresses that, especially on the line I play on with Troy Mallette and Mark Janssens. He really wants us to bang and that's really my type of game and if anybody wants to have fisticuffs, I'm willing to do it with anybody in the league. If anybody is going to run a guy like Brian Leetch or James Patrick, I'll be there. That's my job. As soon as I get out there against that guy I'm going to let him know what he did wrong, and that goes for anybody.

I don't really care about the media credit or anything like that. I know that the players really appreciate what I do and the players tell me that, and the coaches appreciate it and they tell me. That's the whole thing that matters to me and I really don't care what the media says about me or what anybody on the other teams say about me.

When a game starts, I don't usually look at who the referee is because I consider all of them to be the same. It's tough on me because some referees just come into the game thinking, "Hey, this guy's a tough guy, I want him out." Sometimes you get a penalty for your reputation and that bothers me, but I'm just learning. Our coaches, Colin Campbell and Wayne Cashman, help me out a lot and they tell me what to expect of the referees.

If a guy does something to one of my teammates, I'll never forget. If a guy said something to me that really bothered me, I won't forget. But fightingwise, I don't hold grudges. Ken Baumgartner is the tough guy on the Islanders and I'm the tough guy on the Rangers, so people expect us to fight. I don't hold any grudges against the guy and I respect all the tough guys in the league because they have a hard job. They've got to show up every night and if they don't show up, it's not good for them.

I'd say Dave Brown is the toughest guy in the league. Then I'd say Bob Probert, Joey Kocur, Ken Baumgartner, and Troy Crowder. Brown's been such a tough guy and known as the heavyweight champ for so long, and I respect the guy because he's done so much for tough guys in the league and he shows you what a tough guy can do for a team. He's done it in Philadelphia and he's done it in Edmonton, so it shows what a tough guy can bring to a team.

When it comes to fisticuffs, I think the linesmen should let guys fight until they're tired out. These days they just jump as soon as they both stop punching. Fights last 10 to 15 seconds and if you watched a fight five years ago, they'd be going on for two minutes. Those are better to watch and I think they'd be more fun to be in.

My first Ranger fight [with Alan May of the Capitals] gave me some confidence because I knocked him down in my first game. I fought in every preseason game. I did well with each guy that I fought so that gave me a lot of confidence. But I got sent down, so I was pretty disappointed.

You often hear that fighting should be abolished, but if there were no fighting, I don't think hockey would be as popular as it is now. It's the only sport where you can have a full-out fight, fist-to-fist. People pay to see it. Why change it? We fighters are not hurting anyone else.

I don't hate anyone when I fight. I just fight. People say I'm crazy, but I just get joy from fighting. People laugh at me when I laugh at a fight. My teammates say, "Why do you laugh after you fight all the time?" I say, "I don't know, I just laugh."

Chapter 21

KEN BAUMGARTNER
THE PROFESSOR
Speaks Out

As tough guys go, Ken Baumgartner is an anomaly — and if you don't believe it, ask him. "Actually," Baumgartner insists, "I'm a pacifist away from the rink." This comes as no surprise to those who remember Baumgartner, the youth, growing up in Flin Flon, Manitoba, where he was considered one of the brightest youngsters in the mining community.

But as any professional hockey man will attest, there is no direct correlation between office passivity and the behaviour of professional hockey players at the rink. After serving his junior hockey apprenticeship with the Prince Albert Raiders, Baumgartner was signed by the Buffalo Sabres, but was traded to the Los Angeles organization before playing a single game with Buffalo. Ken was assigned to the Kings' New Haven farm club. The awkward six-foot-one, 200-pound defenseman did not immediately impress with his natural hockey prowess, but Baumgartner exuded a joie de hockey that immediately endeared him to both the coaching staff and the New Haven fans. Ken soon caught the attention of Kings general manager Rogie Vachon and was promoted to the big club for 30 games in the 1987–88 season. Despite limited playing time, Baumgartner managed to tally two goals and three assists in addition to 189 penalty minutes — an average of over six minutes per game — and assured himself of at least another look from the general staff.

"Ken was one of my favourite players," says Kings owner Bruce McNall, "both as an individual to deal with and a player to watch. It was very difficult for me to see him traded."

Baumgartner had played parts of the 1988–89 and 1989–90 season when Vachon deemed him expendable. Ken was traded along with centre Hubie McDonough to the New York Islanders on November 29, 1989 for forward Mikko Makela. At the time the trade was made, Islanders general manager Bill Torrey was ridiculed by some members of the media for what they considered a bad move. Makela had been a skilled player who many believed could still be productive. McDonough had been a nondescript minor leaguer who was not expected to add much to the cranky Islanders offense. Few thought much of Baumgartner's competence, particularly since he had been low man on an already defensively weak Los Angeles team.

At the time of the trade, the Islanders were mired deep at the bottom of the Patrick Division with virtually no hope of a playoff berth. Certainly few, if anyone, expected Baumgartner to be a catalyst. Yet the results were astonishing, to say the least. Ken and Hubie made their Islander debut in a game at Chicago Stadium against the always tough Black-hawks. Early in the match, a scrap along the boards developed, with Chicago's Steve Thomas accosting Isles smallish centre Pat LaFontaine. Normally, the Islanders would have been benign in their response. But Baumgartner made a beeline for Thomas and pummelled him before linesmen intervened. The Bomber's response was not lost on the New York bench. The team clearly was revived by his police action and responded with a surprise 2–0 shutout of the Blackhawks.

From that point on, the Islanders went into orbit and eventually climbed from last to first place in the Patrick Division. Certainly, this was not all due to the arrival of Baumgartner, but his belligerence didn't hurt.

"He was a big addition," says coach Al Arbour, "because he gave us muscle and enthusiasm."

However, the Islanders went into a tailspin in the home stretch and just barely made the playoffs on the final night of the season. In the opening game of the Rangers–Islanders playoff Baumgartner's police role backfired after LaFontaine was injured by an elbow dished out by Ranger defenseman James Patrick. In the waning seconds of the contest, Baumgartner and his sidekick Mick Vukota attacked two Rangers. Neither Ranger seemed willing to fight. One, Jeff Bloemberg, tussled and took a beating which later became a cause célèbre with the media. It was pointed out that Bloemberg was a born-again Christian who was religiously opposed to fighting. More devastating to the Islanders was the negative publicity generated by the episode and the fact that Baumgartner was suspended for the series.

Ken returned to the Islanders the following season established as a fan favourite. During the off-season, he had recorded a heavy-metal disc and firmly established himself as a character among NHL enforcers.

His performance was less than positive to the Islanders the second time around. Arbour experimented with Baumgartner as a left wing, *though he mostly played defense through the 1990–91 season. Although he did not have the same impact, he did earn himself a regular position on the team and proved that he could do more than simply throw punches.*

Baumgartner, a student at Hofstra University in the off-season, was interviewed by reporter Linda Lundgren at the Islanders' Cantiague Park practice rink.

Actually, away from the rink I'm not a violent person. I'm actually quite a pacifist. I was the boy who was chased home from school until grade 7 and finally stood up for myself; I beat up four people on the way home from school that day and they left me alone ever since then. I might have had one or two tussles in midget hockey but it wasn't until age sixteen in Flin Flon that I realized I could use this to attain a higher level.

That was actually the first year I wasn't wearing a face mask, also. The way I looked at it, I could use my toughness to attain a higher level. To get there, by playing and practising every day and with better players, you're bound to improve and you have to just keep up. A year later I remember a three-day practice tryout in the middle of October. I had just about, more or less, written off playing Tier One junior. My skills weren't that high then.

The first game was in Saskatoon. I fought Dale Henry and Joey Kocur. I was the seventeen-year-old rookie and at that point I would have done anything to stay. I did pretty well. I cut Hank — I'm not sure if it was a punch or when we hit the ice. The second fight — you have to realize that Kocur was about nineteen or twenty and I was seventeen. The third time he struck my helmet. I said, "Enough of this" and flipped him and fell to the ice. But it was instant acceptance by my teammates because there are a lot of players on hockey teams who appreciate a guy who's going to stick up for them and who's going to be there to look after that role.

In my first year of junior, Terry Simpson kept me out of the situations with the speed flow teams and I wouldn't play against top lines. I wasn't thrown into the fire. We had a pretty tough team, tough reputation, so players like myself would feed off that. I was playing there with Rod Dallman, Dave Manson, and Al Stewart so I wasn't doing it alone. It wasn't like some guys who fight just as much on the ice as they do in the bar. That wasn't my mould. I never really respected players who did that. It seems as if there are two sets of rules. Sometimes the rules on the ice and the rules of society.

There is something called youthful enthusiasm and you don't really think about what you are doing there. By this level (the NHL), you have to have it pretty cut-and-dried. Every time you come to a new level you have to build up a reputation. By my third year, players would leave me alone and the majority of the battles I was fighting were in defense of teammates. The coach was telling me to stay on the ice because I was too valuable to be in the penalty box. That was something great. I was working for that. You have to build your reputation and work to a higher level to that point where they say they need you.

After junior, I went to Europe strictly to improve my skills. I was offered a contract by Los Angeles and I said, "Thank you, but will it still be there in March?" They said yes and gave me their blessing to go to Europe to work on my skills. I played in Chur, Switzerland. It was in their "A" league so it was against their best players. I think it was tougher off the ice than on the ice. Here I am, twenty years old in a foreign country. There was always someone who spoke English so I got by that way. I knew I was there for only six months, I knew I was coming back, and I knew why I was there — to work on my skills. The way I look at it, it saved me six months of brawling in the American Hockey League and I was able to come back in March and accomplish, in the toughness role, in 13 games what it probably would have taken the whole 80 games to accomplish.

My first fight in the American Hockey League was in Newmarket. We didn't have many guys from out West and not a lot of people knew me. They just thought, "Oh here comes this fancy Dan from Europe. What we need now is a tough guy. We don't need any more fancy players." But I surprised a lot of people and once again had instant acceptance. It had been a long year for New Haven; they were lacking that tough role. I ended up playing 13 games and ended up third on the team in penalty minutes.

The next year, I was one of six returning players. Robbie Ftorek was coach. I was like "Holy cow, I can step into one of the veteran roles." I was paired with Kenny Hammond and that worked out really well. Nobody put a lot of responsibility on me with so few games played but the fact was that there was no one else to give it to. I had to continue to make my rounds around the league and continue to build a reputation.

After 35 games, Ftorek was called up to the Kings and took a few players with him. Don Perry came in, made me captain in my second game under him. Kenny Hammond, my partner, wasn't the best fighter in the world. He got blindsided by Rod Dallman in Springfield. I went over and fought Dallman. Perry finds out after the game that Dallman is a friend of mine and he felt that anyone who is going to do that for a teammate can wear the C. Only 45 games in the league and I'm wearing the captain's C.

A little more added responsibility and actually when you are given the C, you tend to excel. It's amazing what a kid can do if some faith is put in him. You see it all around. Some coaches and management can make or break some players with the faith they put in them. By January, I was called up to the NHL.

Shane Churla and I always had a bit of a rivalry with Medicine Hat. We must have fought about a dozen times. And I wasn't the most talented fighter when I began. You bump into someone on the line change, drop your gloves and hold on tight and hope you hit something. After a while, once you establish a reputation, you have to worry a little bit about quality control. You can't have certain people beating you because that eats away at your reputation. Then it is the quality, not the quantity, that becomes the point.

When I came back to New Haven, I hadn't had a fight in one year. There is a reporter in New Haven, John Stein, who would keep fight cards — game, player, TKO, KO, how many stitches, and did he come back into the game. It's nothing I'm proud about, but at the time I thought, "Gee, this is great." There were five or six fights at the end of that season that I did well in and all of a sudden — instant reputation from those five fights, where some guys were working all season for that reputation.

When I came up to pro, my first game was in New Jersey. I took a good run at the Devils' captain, Kirk Muller. I guess I didn't know who anybody was. I didn't know I was not supposed to hit him. Craig Wolanin came after me and we had a big five-on-five in the end.

L.A. had a lot of tough players at the time — Dean Kennedy, Mark Hardy, Jay Wells, Joey Paterson — but they'd been doing it for a long time and what they needed was some young guy to come in with a little reckless abandon, and all of a sudden they thought, "Geez, that's fun again." So in those 30 games I ended up having 20 or 21 fights and I fought some pretty tough players. I fought Bob Probert, Marty McSorley. I always did okay against the bigger players rather than the small, quicker players who would give a big guy a little more trouble. Which reminds me that in my third year of training camp in Prince Albert there was a little guy — I don't even remember his name — who gave me a black eye. The kid didn't even make the team. All the guys let me have it after that. To this day a lot of them don't let me forget that.

In those first 30 games in L.A., much like when I came to the American Hockey League, I stood up to some big players, and I was so happy to be a pro in the NHL that I was playing some of the best hockey of my career, even to this date, on adrenalin alone. On top of that I was establishing myself in the NHL as an enforcer. What was important to me was that I did it from a playing role rather than three shifts a game on the end of the bench, because everyone wants to play and that role as the enforcer is tougher to do going out there cold. Referees know that you're going to try to start something. If you are given a regular shift you are given the benefit of the doubt by the referees.

If you're going out there and taking extra penalties, you may think you are trying to spark the team but you are only hurting the team. But that's something — the regular shift — the player has to earn. I think that in itself has kept some pretty tough players from making it to this level because their skills were not high enough. Even your tough guys these days have very good skills as compared to ten years ago. You can't do below a minimal job for the team defensively. You have to be able to get the puck out of your own end and forwards have to know who their man is coming back. You don't help the team no matter what you can offer in toughness if you can't do those minimal requirements. The way the rules are leaning, your tough guys have to be better and better players.

What I tell the young players coming up is, "Work on your skills" because they're all saying, "Bomber, love your fighting; wish I could fight like you." I say, "No, you don't want to because it's not a life for everyone." I'm forecasting that as the years pass, fighting will play a less significant role in the NHL. I tell kids that if they have pro aspirations — work on your skills. Pattern yourself after Patty LaFontaine, not after me.

I think the willingness to fight is inborn, but it can be an acquired talent. The way I acquired it was through experience. One fights better when angry at something, be it someone offended you or one of your teammates. It is much easier to fight for a cause rather than go out and feel forced into it or feel you have to. I feel lucky that I never had a coach tell me to go out and fight someone because I think if I did it would take any joy out of it that I could derive.

To win a fight, don't get hit and if you don't get hit, change hands. Different players have different techniques. Most tie down, some don't and hope their sweater gets pulled off, leaving their opponent nothing to hold on to and they're free to swing away. Without going into giving any of my secrets away, some people watch a lot of fight tapes and some scout the other team's tough guys — much like a goal scorer scouts a goaltender.

About a third of the players you can intimidate by your presence. Another third can be intimidated if you growl at them a bit, and a third of the players in the league you are not going to intimidate regardless. But you definitely *can* intimidate. It is much more effective when the enforcer is involved in the game in a regular aspect, a regular shift, rather than being out there once or twice a period. Then the opposition says, "Just leave him alone; don't wake him up." The referees know the enforcer is out there to start something and then he's in the penalty box — takes a bad penalty — and he doesn't play again. Intimidation is much more effective when you can contribute regularly.

Mentally, 80 games is a long season, and you have to realize that even if you don't want to mix it up that night you always have to be aware that someone on the other team might, so you can't let your guard down at any one moment. There are times when the other team may play without an enforcer and you don't have to worry about that aspect that much. There aren't too many guys who play the role into their thirties; just a few like Jay Miller, Chris Nilan. These guys have been around for quite some time and they're still doing their job.

Physically, there is very little pain and the pain doesn't hurt. A few stitches never hurt anyone. It may look painful, but. . .

What amazes me about all the critics of fighting is where they were in the 1970s when Philadelphia used intimidation to win Stanley Cups. We have no more bench-clearing brawls in the sport. You can't say that for basketball and for baseball. Very seldom in hockey is it more than a one-on-one confrontation. Very seldom is it a situation where one player is outmatched by the other. You don't see guys who are six foot four fighting guys five foot ten unless the guy five-ten wants to. Most enforcers pride themselves upon being "fair fighters" — if there is such a word. What it is is the game has never been cleaner, yet there has never been such an uproar against fighting in hockey. Maybe they're right, maybe they're wrong — time will tell.

Chapter 22

MARTY McSORLEY

GRETZKY'S BODYGUARD

Speaks Out

To this day, the Pittsburgh Penguins are kicking themselves for mis-reading Marty McSorley's ability. The Hamilton, Ontario native was signed as a free agent by the Penguins in 1982 and played 72 games for Pittsburgh as an NHL rookie in the 1983–84 season.

While his style was crude — he totalled 224 penalty minutes — there was an exuberance about him that should have signalled the Pittsburgh high command that they had a winner. The Penguins employed McSorley in only 15 games during the 1984–85 campaign and traded him to Edmonton in September 1985. Marty played on the 1987 and 1988 Oilers Stanley Cup winners and demonstrated that he was much more than a tough guy. During the 1987 Cup run, he had four goals and three assists in 21 playoff games.

When Edmonton traded Wayne Gretzky to Los Angeles in June 1989, Gretzky insisted that McSorley be included in the deal. It was a for-tuitous move for the Kings. McSorley, who had alternated between forward and defense, was moved permanently to the back line. His play improved during the year and in 1990–91 he had become one of the most reliable members of the Kings' blueline brigade.

The change did not alter Marty's outlook on the opposition. He remained supremely intense and as truculent as he had been during his rookie season. He also blossomed into one of the league's most ebullient, eloquent, and amusing personalities. He was interviewed at the Great Western Forum by Los Angeles correspondent Joel Bergman.

I grew up in a family of seven boys; I have six brothers. I grew up in the small town of Cayuga, about 25 miles south of Hamilton and about an hour and a half from Buffalo, where everything was basically geared towards hockey. We played softball and different things, but hockey was it. The Leafs were on TV on Wednesday and Saturday night, and sometimes we got the Canadiens. We would rarely get to see Bobby Orr and the Bruins, Gordie Howe, and Bobby Hull, but they were really big then and they were exciting guys. We wanted to be like them and we dreamt about playing in the NHL. Growing up on the farm with my brothers, getting into the NHL wasn't taken for granted. It wasn't easy and doors didn't open all of a sudden to us. The guys that came out of the small towns really had to work hard; they had to really want it because we had to basically move away from home at a young age to get to a level or calibre of play that was competitive enough for us to move on.

My career as enforcer began when I played Junior D, both my years of midget when I was fifteen and sixteen. That was a tough league because it had teams with mainly nineteen- and twenty-year old guys, and I was only fifteen. Many of them were big farm boys and played the old style of hockey. Everybody on the ice had the ability to fight and look after themselves. When you're fifteen, you are no different from the other guys, and my three brothers wouldn't let me back down from anybody. Growing up, my brothers and I were very competitive. Each one of us had to stand up for ourselves. My older brother Paul made sure of that. We used to go along with the old saying on the farm, "If it doesn't hurt, you don't cry," even at a young age. If you got into a spat, when the spat was over you went back to work.

When I moved away at the age of seventeen, I used to drive into Hamilton to play Junior B. I was rough around the edges. I was tall and a bit awkward. I knew I had to hit and take the body and really be physical, but there wasn't any fighting. The league instituted a rule that if you were fighting, they would throw you out of the game. I only had a couple of fights that year, but I was physical.

I was on the third and fourth lines there, but as the year went on I improved. I think I had the ability to improve more because I hadn't been in the calibre of play that a lot of those guys had been. Then I got a tryout with Belleville, which was an expansion franchise. John Mowat invited me to the camp in Belleville where Larry Mavety was the coach. John came behind the bench, patted me on the back the second day of camp and said, "They need your size on this hockey club." At that time I didn't need much prodding to fight, a little push and shove here and there. I wasn't scared to mix it up. Mavety was showing me that there were defined roles for some players — that maybe there wasn't as much of everybody looking after their own battles, as a few guys looked after most of the guys' battles. I took that upon myself. In that year, I didn't play a lot, but I was ready, willing, and able at any time to mix it up if anything happened.

Then as an eighteen-year-old, I tried out for Major A just on an invite when most kids were drafted at seventeen. I grew a lot later than a lot of other guys. I was 207 pounds when I broke into the league and I'm now 230 pounds. I was still growing at the age of twenty-one, twenty-two, twenty-three, still filling out. John might have made it a little more obvious to me but I knew the game was physical. I knew that Major A would have a lot of fighting because I had seen it before. He made it more obvious that fewer guys fought for more guys, that not everybody looked after themselves.

I was always a defenseman, all the way through junior and in my first year at Pittsburgh. In my second season with the Penguins Bob Berry moved me up to right wing for the first 15 games, but it was only for one or two shifts a game. I really didn't know the position, although it was basically to be a tough guy. Then I went back to the minors and played defense for the whole year. In Edmonton they said they were going to make me into a right wing. But it was a defined role that they wanted me to play, but to be tough. They wanted me to work hard, keep my mouth shut, and be a good team member. I think there, more than anywhere, they really stressed that you had to have a strong character for the hockey team. Your character and your personality had to match with everybody else on the hockey club. Being a tough guy, you're a piece of the puzzle, a little bit of the chemistry of the hockey club. So they said that if I was going to be a right winger, the guys on the team genuinely wanted me to be a better player. They wanted to work with me, and were as happy as I was when I scored or made a move. Glen Sather wouldn't say anything, but he'd let me know if I screwed up, tried to be too fancy, or let being a player get in the way of being a tough guy. There were times when he'd come up and say that I wasn't born with a great pair of hands, or I shouldn't be in the neutral zone, or different things like that; simply to let me know not to get away from the job that's got to help the hockey club. But at the same time he put me on the ice to play. He let me practise on a line with Mark Messier and Glenn Anderson. Why was I practising with those guys? To get me skating.

I am thankful to be in L.A. I came down here being an experienced hockey player. Down here to be a strong team player you have got to be tough. But I did it not from a personal sense but from a team sense. I've never really asked Wayne Gretzky if he specifically asked for me to be included in the trade to L.A. When I heard Wayne was going to L.A., it really upset me because God knows what Wayne does to a hockey team. At that time we had lost Paul Coffey, Reijo Ruotsalainen, and Kent Nilsson and I was really upset. Then to hear that Wayne was going — wow! I really believe Wayne had influence in my being down here, but you also know too that Edmonton's not going to give up Mark Messier, Kevin Lowe, Glenn Anderson or Grant Fuhr. But for Wayne to think of me in that sense, yes, that was a good feeling. That's a hell of a good feeling. That tells me that the job that I did in Edmonton was appreciated. When I was playing up there, the guys let you know that they appreciated you. It was another little boost to think that management in L.A. and Wayne thought highly enough of me to ask to have me involved.

Two things helped me as a player. One was Larry Mavety, my coach at Belleville. When I first started there I didn't play much. But because he knew that I was willing to get my nose dirty, he kept me working. He kept me around because I worked hard and wanted to play. Also he had an influence on me because when I played rotten, he kept playing me. He didn't keep me in that tough-guy role. He let me develop as a player. A lot of guys get stuck into a tough-guy role and are unable to get away from it.

The second thing was playing for Edmonton. It helped me a tremendous amount. I went to a very, very talented hockey team. I played with players who were tremendously talented, and I had the ability to improve as a player. I had the ability to go out and play with great players and watch them. That's where, more than anywhere, I developed a real love of the game. I was a fan because I played with great guys and I had a chance to see how things were done and I could see how the game was with superstars.

It helped to see great players and how the game was broken down, how it was played at a high level and all the things that were done behind the scenes. It improved my game tremendously because I had the chance to improve and to watch firsthand all of that and try to incorporate some of it into my game. I knew that I couldn't incorporate all of the things that Mark Messier does or all the things Jari Kurri does or all the things Wayne Gretzky does. But little bits and pieces I could pick up. I learned to read the game better. As a tough guy I learned when to fight and when not to fight. I learned there are times when you've got to take a punch in the face, there are times when it's important not to take a penalty, and times when it's important to push back for the team. A tough guy had to work hand in hand with the other 19 guys on the bench and on the ice. You are a piece of the puzzle. You would want a guy out there fighting your battles and letting him take a penalty sometimes.

I didn't get that feeling in Pittsburgh. Mario Lemieux wasn't there. He was there my second year, but I only played 15 games my second year. Then I was sent to the minors for the rest of the year. Every time I think about that trade from Pittsburgh I thank Eddie Johnston. Eddie put me in a position to go to Edmonton. Even when Eddie phoned me, he said, "I think I'm putting you in a place where you can play," because it was a very defined role in Edmonton. It's tough being a tough guy on a bad hockey team because you're on the fourth line that doesn't play. There's no room to be a tough guy when you're losing hockey games, because you've got to get goals. You can't afford to take any time because you're not winning any hockey games. You're always fighting from behind, so it's tough. I think when you lose sometimes, it's because you're not tough enough. The tough guy hasn't been able to play and his hands are cuffed a lot of the time. That's a very tough role. On a good hockey team you often have a two- or three-goal lead, so you can afford to play a tough guy. Sometimes the tough guy will get a penalty, and if a team is good enough that they could still win, they're good enough that they can absorb and kill the penalty.

You don't make someone into a tough guy. That comes from within. You don't take a big kid and say, "Okay, you're gonna be a tough guy because you have all the physical attributes to do it." You have to have that Sutter type of mentality that you can go nose-to-nose no matter what. It doesn't matter who; just play hard. If you don't have it from within, sooner or later you are going to take a whopping. Tough guys will come back. Players that aren't tough won't come back.

If I had been in a stronger hockey program at a younger age and become a goal scorer, I don't think I would have had as many fights. But I certainly wouldn't have been looking for somebody else to fight any of my battles. There would have been fewer fights, but then you get into a very delicate situation about what's best for the hockey team.

If you are a goal scorer like Mark Messier, you may be able to fight, but you don't want him to fight more than once a game because it's not good for the hockey club. That's where the tough guy has to step in and be the guy that goes out and does that role and lets Mark Messier play hockey. That's a sensitive thing that has to be thought out around the hockey club. Even as a tough guy you have to have some rules. I have some rules I live by. One of them is fight on my time. There may be times it looks like I backed down. But if I'm at the end of a minute-and-a-half shift, where I am caught out there on the blueline and some guy comes over and instantly drops the stick, it doesn't make sense to fight him. I'll be back out on the ice and I'm going to make it square.

Another thing is when you're up two goals, it's not as good for the hockey team to be fighting as much. If they take liberties with some of your goal scorers, then maybe you have to step up. When you get up three or four goals, teams have a tendency to get chippy. Then maybe a fight is necessary to keep the game from getting too chippy and to keep the other team honest.

I think what's happening now is that teams are realizing that tough guys are no good on the bench. They have got to be able to be on the ice. Now if I go and fight, and I'm gone or if I get kicked out of the game, my tough teammate Jay Miller is probably gonna be playing more than he maybe would have. Saying nothing against Jay, but he's probably going to play more just to keep that physical presence on the ice more often. And it's up to one or two guys to do it.

When I first broke into the league, a couple of fights stand out. We went to Philly and lost 11-3. I had two fights that night — with Dave

Brown and Daryl Stanley. I didn't have to fight that night, but I did because I didn't want to lose and felt bad about losing. As I look back on it, I think that's the way I always have to think. No matter how bad you're losing you never give up. No matter what the situation looks like, the other guys on the team have to know that you're not quitting and won't quit under any circumstances, because you're not going to want to let that get infectious and carry into other games. I will always remember that you can have a direct influence on all the other guys with fighting.

I also remember another fight from that year. It was with Mark Messier as I came out of the penalty box. It was my first year in the league. That could have had a direct relationship with my being traded to Edmonton, because they knew that I was going to come back and keep coming back.

I remember two fights as an Oiler — one with Gord Donnelly simply because he had wiped out Mike Krushelnyski's knee. I went over immediately and started to fight. It was my first year there, but I think I let the guys know that I was in it for them. It was personal because one of our guys was injured and I was going to do whatever I could about it to protect our guys.

Another one I remember was with Jim Kyte in a playoff game against Winnipeg in my second year with Edmonton, the first time I won a Cup. We were playing in Edmonton for the second game of the series. I didn't do too badly in the fight. I think we got two or three goals following the fight, and I learned that there are times when you can really pick the guys up. I was in a very specified role there, as being more of a physical player helped the hockey team.

My job as a player here in Los Angeles has changed a lot because right now the fighting has changed. There's not nearly as much fighting. You've got fewer guys who fight on each team. I think the game has improved now where you put a guy on the ice who's a fighter and he'd better be able to play because if not, the five guys from the other team are talented enough to take advantage of that. It used to be if you had a player on the ice like that you didn't capitalize on him as much, but right now they'll burn him. What you've got is that they look down upon players like that and the penalties are much stiffer. It seems that there isn't as much intimidating physically as there used to be. There's a lot of hitting but there's not the threat of five or six guys in the lineup who are going to take a swing at somebody.

In my first couple of years when a guy needed a spanking they gave him a shot or two and you got four or five minutes. Now they give you a game misconduct without even thinking about it. Last season, against Edmonton, I went in to celebrate a goal — didn't say a word to anybody — then Tony Granato was dumped and I got ten minutes called. Basically, they're making it tough to go after a guy.

If you're not playing a lot, it doesn't matter how many minutes in penalties you get because you're still doing your job. If I'm playing a lot and I'm one of six defensemen and they use me for killing penalties, it's tough for me and the hockey club.

There are instances when you have to do that, where a ten-minute misconduct is needed to do something protective for the hockey club. But to get a cheap misconduct, when it doesn't do anybody any good, it just puts an extra weight on the other guys. You really have to decide how important it is and how effective the job you did is.

It's interesting now that I am playing more that some of the guys who don't play that much come out looking to fight me, and I'm thinking of the game and I'm not physically prepared to battle those guys. I've got to give myself a minute or two to regroup and then come back on the ice. Then the heat of the moment is lost.

Some people misinterpret it, thinking that maybe you've backed down or you've chickened out. It's not pretty out there; you can get injured. You don't go into it looking to dance. You want to punch a guy. You've got to be prepared to go in there to do that. I don't want to go into a fight and embarrass myself. I'd rather come back and fight again.

There are times before a game I have a feeling that it is going to be a very physical hockey game. The chances are very good that I'm going to get into a fight. You go into the game and think that there's one or two guys you're going to be fighting with. But there's nobody I'm going into the game with and say, "Okay, I'm going to go after him." I go into a game thinking the game is going to present itself. If we jump out to a two-goal lead, it's foolish for me to go and get into a fight unless something really provokes it.

If I go looking for somebody, that's selfish. There's no room for that. If you get down a goal or two and they're taking the play to you, there's maybe a guy or two that you can be physical with to give the team confidence and get them going. That's an instance where you know who to go to. If I'm going to go out and make an impact on the game, I have to slow down the guy who's flying. My going out and fighting the big guy isn't going to slow down the little guy. So I punish the little guy. If he comes down my side and I'm the defenseman, punish him. Maybe when he goes to pick the puck up next time he's going to look over his shoulder and that's to our benefit.

It's basic intimidation to kind of run somebody out of the game, knock him around and get him so stiff that he doesn't want to play, keep him honest so he doesn't have a sense of controlling the game. I'm not saying beating the hell out of them. If he comes down my side I'm going to hit him within the rules.

If another team wants to think of me as a goon, let them go right ahead. As long as the referee on the ice doesn't think of me as a goon, it's nice. There are times when you are going to get the old "just get them off the ice so nothing happens." I hate those calls because I want to play.

I hate a cheap call, and they do happen. You can't imagine how many times; because the game has gotten chippy and the referee said, "That McSorley's not kosher," or two guys are fighting and the linesmen turn and grab you. That can lead to a lot of bad calling.

You've got to be emotional, because if you go in there lackadaisical you are going to get hurt. You can't go in there thinking that this is a nine-to-five job and I'm going to go about my business. You have got to be in there and you have to be sharp. You've got to keep your head up and you have to be perfectly aware of what the other guy is doing because there are guys who want to hurt you. After a fight I have a high. When I go to the penalty box, my adrenalin is pumped. Sometimes if I didn't feel I did so well I want to get right back out there and get a piece of you again. Other times when you come back to the bench the guys are proud of you and they tell you so. There are times when a fight can take my game out, but most of the time I feel a notch above where I was before the fight.

Chapter 23

CRAIG BERUBE
THE BROAD STREET BULLY, 1990s STYLE

Speaks Out

If there was any question about the genuine toughness of Craig Berube, it was dispelled easily in the 1990–91 season. At the time the Philadelphia Flyers' left wing, the six-foot-two, 205-pounder from Calihoo, Alberta had seen two of his heavyweight teammates physically embarrassed by enforcer Troy Crowder of the New Jersey Devils. In the first bout, Crowder demolished Flyers defenseman Jeff Chychrun, breaking Chychrun's nose. Next in line was forward Tony Horacek, one of the league's better fighters. It was no contest. Horacek was boxed into submission. At that point, it would have been understandable if the Flyers had dropped any belligerent designs on Crowder, for purposes of personal health if nothing else. That, however, did not take into account Berube's special courage. The next time the Devils and Flyers met, Craig sought out Crowder and unhesitatingly exchanged lefts and rights until they were separated by the linesmen. The verdict was at the very worst a draw, although some observers suggested that Berube was the winner on points. That, of course, is academic. What really mattered is that Berube had the guts to take a physical stand with the personality who, at the time, was one of the most feared fighters in the league.

Craig's ascent to a regular position was typical for a player of his modest talents. He auditioned with the Flyers in 1986–87, coming directly to the NHL from the junior amateur ranks of the Western Hockey League. He played seven games for Philadelphia in his rookie season, as well as five playoff games. His goals, assists, and point totals, right across the board, were 0–0–0. However, true to his profession, he accumulated 57 regular-season penalty minutes and 17 more in the Stanley Cup round.

Unsure about his big-league ability, the Flyers general staff put Berube on a belt line to their Hershey farm team in 1987–88 and again in 1988–89. His play significantly improved each year — he played 27 NHL games in his second season and 53 in his third — and by 1989–90, Craig had won a full-time varsity berth with the Flyers. He played in 74 games, scoring 4 goals with 14 assists, for 18 points. His 291 penalty minutes attested to his belligerence.

Berube had hoped that his vigorous effort would earn him a new contract with Philadelphia, but incoming (1990–91) general manager Russ Farwell refused to negotiate a new deal with Berube's agent, Larry Rauch, and Craig finished the campaign uncertain about his NHL future.

In that regard Craig was typical of the fringe player whose forte was fighting. There was no question that Craig had improved his skill level over a period of five seasons, nor was there doubt about his fearlessness. The only questions that remained centred around further improvement as a player and his salary growth. "We know that he'll get a job," says Rauch. "The only question is where." During the summer of 1991 he was dealt to Edmonton.

I was kind of the bad kid. I would start stuff and pick on people. I was bigger than most people. A couple of times I got a licking from my older cousins for getting out of hand. We were fighting all the time. Even as I grew up in Williams Lake, British Columbia I used to do a lot of fighting off the ice, too.

My father and uncles were aggressive. They were involved with that kind of stuff and they played hockey. They played rough, tough hockey. When I was in Williams Lake, a guy named John Van Horic taught me how to be tough, play tough and fight on the ice. He was a big part of my career today. He was a real mean coach and I owe him a lot. He taught me how to be a man at an early age. He had me boxing and all that stuff and he made me do things that I didn't want to do. I didn't want to fight on the ice, but he made me and it taught me.

The first half of the year I never fought very much or anything. The second half he really was on me to get involved in that kind of situation. I was a big kid and I wasn't a great player and he knew that I wanted to play.

In my first fight, I was so scared that I just hammered the guy. It was in Tier Two, Williams Lake. I just started swinging and I hit him, I hit him, I hit him and gave it to him good. He was noted to be a pretty tough guy and it gave me a lot of confidence.

Mike Keenan called me up to the Flyers during my first year in the minors and it was with about one month left in the season. I did some fighting and I just stayed. Keenan likes that style and I did whatever he wanted me to do or whatever it took for the team to win.

I like a lot of tough guys but I never modelled my style of play after anyone. I think I've got my own style. I just do what's right at the time.

I enjoy the lifestyle of hockey. Sometimes I don't enjoy it when I know I have to fight. It's hard thinking about it all day, but I've learned over the years not to let it bother me as much. When I was younger it used to affect me. I don't have the fear of being beaten up but it bothers me to lose a fight.

One night I got a beating from Lyndon Byers. I never forgot it. I thought I was done after that, but I had to go back and do it again. I've never been beaten like that before. When you lose a fight like that, you lose your confidence. But you blow it off and just go back at it and do the job.

After the Byers fight, my next fight was in the minors. I think it was one of the Dineens. I was a little cautious and I wasn't myself. I slowly worked my way back. I have been beaten after that and it doesn't bother me at all.

Tough play is the only way I'm going to play, and it's a good role. It's a big part of the game. It's my job and I like playing in the National Hockey League. I know I've improved my skills, but I still have to do my role — to play hard and a lot of hitting and that kind of stuff. I like it. I was treated really well in Philadelphia and I liked my role and I like what I did for the hockey team.

My mom doesn't like fighting. She's always saying not to fight, but she knows I've gotta. My father doesn't say too much about it. He knows it's my role and he accepts it.

We used to do a lot of boxing. I was really good at boxing, so I fought some amateur fights. I won a couple and thought I was tough. I thought of boxing professionally but I do it in the summer for training. It gives a lot of wind and it's hard work and builds muscles. It's good training.

Troy Crowder is a good fighter. He's big and throws his punches fast. He's smart, he waits, he comes in and grabs you and slugs right away. He's got a powerful punch. He's a smart fighter. I can't go in there really stupid and swing with him. I have to battle with him because he's bigger than I am. I have to duck, get inside on him and have fast hands.

I had a pretty good fight with Marty McSorley a few years ago. It was a long one. I've had a few good ones with Bob Probert. Those two, along with Byers, stand out. I've also had a few good fights with Ken Baumgartner.

I think fighting is part of the game and a good part of the game. A good fight toe-to-toe is good. If you take fighting out of the game a lot of guys are going to cheap-shot, but they've got the rules and they're going to do what they want to do.

When a guy comes up and tries to entice me, I just laugh about it and say, "Hey man, see you later." That's another thing I've matured about. When I was younger, I would start to swing.

Balance is a big thing. I try to grab the guy's right arm in a certain place if he is a righty so he can't punch me. For different fighters, I do different things.

Chapter 24

TROY CROWDER

THE HEAVYWEIGHT CHALLENGER AND ALMOST CHAMPION

Speaks Out

Troy Crowder is vivid proof that a player of marginal skills can become an overnight sensation if he handles his dukes the right way at the right time. At the end of the 1989–90 season, Crowder wasn't even dressed by New Jersey Devils' coach John Cunniff and was considered to have a limited future.

When Troy came to training camp in September 1990, Cunniff decided to employ him on a regular line with veteran Laurie Boschman and Al Stewart. Crowder leaped from obscurity in the Devils' home opener against the Detroit Red Wings. He took on Bob Probert, who had been regarded as the league's heavyweight champion, and dispatched the Red Wing to the showers with a bloodied face that required stitches. Just two fights later — after decisive victories over Craig Coxe and Jeff Chychrun — Crowder was obtaining as much attention as Wayne Gretzky.

At times, Crowder looked competent enough to take a regular turn, especially when working on a line with Boschman and Stewart. But when the Devils suffered a crippling slump after the New Year, the line was disassembled and Crowder saw only spot duty. His lustre as a heavyweight contender also diminished after Darin Kimble, then with Quebec, staggered Troy and dropped him to his knees during a game at Byrne Arena.

Whether it was a coincidence or not, the Kimble encounter marked the beginning of the end as far as Crowder's season as a productive Devil was concerned.

The team, which had aspirations for first place on New Year's Day, now found itself in a life-and-death struggle for a playoff berth. Coach Cunniff, who had extracted considerable potential from Crowder earlier in the season, began experiencing personal traumas as the Devils floundered. The coup de grâce for Crowder coincided with the demise of Cunniff as coach. He was fired shortly before the NHL trade deadline in March and replaced by veteran minor league coach Tom McVie.

Unlike Cunniff, whose quiet disposition was similar to Crowder's, McVie was a raucous, no-nonsense type who had briefly coached Crowder in the minors.

No sooner had McVie assumed command than the word was out that Crowder would get even less ice than before. Which is precisely what happened.

This is not an indictment of McVie. His team continued to struggle and the coach groped for a winning combination. Crowder did not help his case with what appeared to be indolent play. When the Devils made their final bid for a playoff berth, Crowder was in civvies. Instead of Crowder, McVie moved energetic Doug Brown into a right-wing slot along with Boschman and Pat Conacher. The unit immediately jelled and turned into one of the Devils' more effective lines. Crowder became a forgotten man. New Jersey squeezed into fourth place and opened the playoffs against the Pittsburgh Penguins.

Once again fate was working against Crowder. The Penguins were virtually a goon-free team, which meant the Devils had little use for Crowder in their series with Pittsburgh.

The Brown–Boschman–Conacher unit proved to be the most consistent in the seven-game series. Crowder never was dressed and there were few "play Crowder" cries from the crowd. The Devils' loss to the Penguins ended a season that had as many pluses and minuses for the club as a whole as it did for Troy. The club fluctuated from Stanley Cup contenders to dismal underachievers. Likewise, Crowder went from a major headliner, who also contributed to the Devils' early surge, to a virtually useless wingman who was deemed no better than a bench warmer by his new coach. During the summer he was claimed as a free agent by Detroit and signed a $350,000 contract.

Whether Troy can ever have a more meaningful season than 1990–91 is a moot question. We know he can handle his dukes and that he is capable, in spots, of delivering modest NHL contributions. But whether he can — or even has the desire to — play hard over the long haul remains to be seen.

Reporters Lou Villano and Matt Messina covered Crowder's rise and fall from the beginning of the 1990–91 season through its conclusion. Villano handled two lengthy interviews with Crowder, and both Villano and Messina talked with him on other occasions. Crowder's words *follow, as well as a postscript on his unusual roller-coaster ride through the NHL's heavyweight division.*

I had a tough year during the 1988–89 season. I wasn't enjoying myself. I was in Utica to develop but I wasn't getting the ice time that I wanted and I wasn't playing as well as I should have. It was just a bad year all around for me.

When I came back the following year in training camp I just had all those negative thoughts with me and I wasn't feeling like I was contributing. I didn't feel good about myself or what I was doing so I said, "Hey, I ain't gonna go through another year of not enjoying it." I took about five months off, but I kept in contact with the Devils. They called me every couple of weeks to ask if I was ready to come back. At that time, I thought I wasn't going to come back.

Hockey was totally off my mind for that whole time, and finally with about two months left in the season Lou Lamoriello said, "I gotta know now; we're getting near the trading deadline, we're getting near the end of the season. Will you do it?" I talked with my dad and he said, "There's two months left and the playoffs, how bad can it be? Go back and try it; if you don't like it, it's only two months, and if you do like it, you know the time off helped you and you can play again."

I went back to the Devils and for a while I really enjoyed myself. The guys were great and really supportive. I just kept improving and even though I didn't play at the end I was feeling good so when I got home that summer of 1990 I said, "You know, I think I can play this game for a long time." I just worked hard and came back with a really good attitude the following year.

Hockey is a great job. The pay is there and then it's a matter of whether you like your job. I like hockey, but I like it when I feel like I'm helping and belonging. A tough guy is supposed to be an important part of the team, but I don't feel that way. I want to contribute. I want to be a player. I want to be on the ice not getting scored against and I want to have chances to score.

Coach Cunniff was really supportive of what I did. He wasn't afraid to tell me what I was doing wrong, but he was the kind of guy who told me when I was doing things right, too. I got better with every game. People told me so.

I don't mind that the public sees me as an enforcer. It's how they saw me before and that's how they see me now. Sure, it's my job, but the other part of my game began going well.

The game has changed. You don't see too many people coming up who are just fighters or scrappers anymore. They like all-around players. It's just a bonus when you're tough, but you can't be just a tough player in this league anymore. All of the guys can play; all of them are getting ice time now. Every tough guy I know in the league is playing a regular shift. I think that's important for the game and it helps the guys who play that role. They say, "I can play a regular shift and be a tough guy."

It takes just a few years to establish yourself as a tough player. Sure, you've got to fight once in a while, but guys become hesitant about taking me on. They figure, "What if he gives me one of those one-punches and knocks me out for a couple of months?" It's more of just a warning. It's like growing up and if I do something wrong my dad's going to give me a spanking or something, so you learn. The respect happens; it doesn't take very long, maybe a couple of years. Five years from now I'll definitely have enough respect and when I can play the game even more, the team will be better off for it.

Because 1990–91 was my first full year, I was on and off. There was still some improving for me to do. The guys on the team knew I was there to take care of anything that happened. The first year had the most fighting for me. That was good for the team because the more I fight, the more assured they will become, and the more confidently they will play.

At the rate of fighting I did I wouldn't have a left hand left. I'm sure that five years from now I'll still have to fight once in a while but it will be just a matter of reputation. That goes a long way in this league.

When I fought Bob Probert the first time, it was a combination of me pulling him closer into me and him pulling back not to get hit. Finally his shirt popped back and then I grabbed for his arm, but at that time the linesmen jumped in, so who knows what would've happened after that. If I would've had more shots at him, it would have been a matter of positioning myself so that I could get shots in and not get hit at the same time.

The first Probert fight helped my reputation. I knew I'd fight more often because of it — and I did. A lot of guys wanted to try me just to see. I knew that if I beat them all I'd have a great reputation and it would be good for my future. After all, a fight doesn't take but ten or thirty seconds.

Fights are tiring when you finish. That's why I try to make them as short as possible. I try to hit hard and fast right off the bat. Sometimes they're long, but not too often. If you get into one or two fights a game, or one every couple of games, it takes only a minute out of the game and a couple of minutes in the penalty box.

For me to stop a fight early it depends who I'm fighting and what they've done. Some guys will eye-gouge you, cheap-shot you after the whistle, and when the linesmen aren't in there will try and hit you. In that situation I'll give it right back to them. If someone is going to claw out my face while I'm lying underneath the referee, then the next time I'm fighting with him I'll knee him in the head when he's down. For some guys the fight's over when they let go and skate away. That's when I do the same thing.

When I fought Jeff Chychrun of the Flyers the ref said, "Stop, he's hurt," and I did because he's a clean fighter. He's not the kind of guy who cheap-shots you. If he wants to fight you he'll challenge you, he'll drop the gloves. That's the way I fight. When he was hurt and down, the fight was over and I stopped. If someone fights fair with me, I'll fight fair with them.

How did I get to fight so well? I worked out the previous summer. I worked out a lot on my leg power and I worked on my upper body strength. I have a heavy bag at home and I hit it a lot. The more I worked on my upper body strength, the harder I hit the bag.

I was kidding with a buddy I work out with. "I'm gonna kill somebody this year. Look at this," I said, and I hit the bag and it shattered. I would break somebody's jaw if I hit them that hard. I don't worry about it because when I get in a fight the first thing I think is, "Hit him as hard as you can and stop him." I guess that's a little bit of fear. I guess it's that I'd rather hit him before he hits me.

It's easier to get hurt in boxing. There's no holding, it's just swing, swing, swing. Kenny Baumgartner's broken a few people's jaws. I've knocked out three or four people in my career. I've also broken a couple of noses. I've hit guys in the eye so hard that they couldn't see out of it for two or three weeks. You can get hurt, but I don't think as much as in boxing.

My first year before junior hockey, two of my friends who were in the OHL for a year were boxing in town, so they said, "If you're gonna go in the league you're gonna have to fight." I never fought when I was a kid, but I was always bigger than everybody else. I went there a few times, sparred, learned how to hit the heavy bag and speed bag, and learned pretty quickly. I found it easy and some of the staff there were impressed with how quickly I learned and how well I could hit the bag and other things. So we sparred a few times and the guy said I should pursue boxing and that it was three years until the Olympics. They said they knew people who could connect me, but I had gotten ahead in the OHL and I wanted to see how hockey would go. I played hockey that year and ended up not boxing, but I did well for myself fighting in hockey. The next summer I went to Belleville, and they have a really good boxing program there during the season.

As for the Olympics, I've always wanted to be in them, since I was a kid. Growing up, I've watched them, and to me, it's the ultimate, it's such an elite crew of younger people who are just starting to find out what they're made of. To me, winning a gold medal in the Olympics would be the ultimate.

The difference between boxing and hockey fighting is that in a hockey fight you're holding on and you're using the body leverage, you're using the holding to prevent his punch from coming, because you don't have that mobility on the ice. The actual punch itself is similar. Like when I hit the bag, I twist my hips, I twist my knees, I throw everything into the punch, and I do the same thing on the ice. So if I'm gonna get in a fight on the ice, I'm gonna make it worthwhile.

Sometimes fighting gets overused but hey, that's North American hockey; that's the way it's played. I think fighting should be used for when someone starts using their stick or cheap-shotting. You can't turn around and say, "Well, I'm gonna sue you because you cross-checked me" or something. You've got to take your frustrations out some way, so you fight, and I believe in it that way.

I don't worry about whether I'm heavyweight champion or not. I've never worried about that. I like people to know that I'm one of the best, anyway, that if they're gonna deal with me, you know, they might get hurt, they might get hurt bad, and that makes my job easier, when people know that.

I have always felt I had the talent to play this game. I've always adapted to sports really easily, and athletically I know I can play. It's just a matter of my confidence level. It's only gonna get better, and I'm only gonna get better.

Postscript on Troy Crowder, 1990–91

Crowder, justifiably, thought he would get better, but this certainly was not the case as the 1990–91 season moved into the home stretch.

All the good things that had happened to him in the first half of the campaign seemed to evaporate, and his productivity was virtually nil.

The demise of Crowder, the hockey player, was carefully observed by reporter Matt Messina, who delivers the following requiem for a hockey heavyweight, 1990–91.

The reputation of a hockey enforcer rests almost exclusively on his latest performance with his fists. If you don't think so, just ask Bob Probert, who suffered through three months with the title of "ex-heavyweight champ" hung upon him after his loss to Crowder on opening night at the Meadowlands. The worth of a Probert or Crowder over the course of a season is usually determined by an evaluation of his fights, and the extent to which he is capable of intimidating the opposition.

Crowder was undefeated through the first half of the season, and very few players dared even to challenge him after his decisive early victories over the likes of Probert, Chychrun, and Horacek. Though he was always composed and soft-spoken, his confidence was unmistakable. When asked about the well-known fighters around the league, Crowder would simply say, "Nobody really worries me."

His hockey skills had improved under coach John Cunniff, who let Crowder play a regular shift with linemates Al Stewart and Laurie Boschman, two very physical players in their own right. "My confidence is getting better," said Crowder after scoring three goals in two games in October. "I have to thank Cunny for that. I never got this much playing time since I was in midget hockey." Even in Detroit, home of the "ex-champ," Cynthia Lambert (Detroit *News*) compared

Crowder favourably to the deposed Probert, praising the Devils' mix of "talent and brawn."

Crowder suffered his first loss of the season on January 24 to Darin Kimble, then of Quebec. Kimble, anxious to establish himself as an enforcer, simply challenged Crowder outright. After an indecisive beginning, Kimble rocked Crowder with a right hand, ending the fight. The Devil would later claim that he had had difficulty getting psyched up for the bout.

Whatever the reason for the loss, it happened at the worst possible time. Only four days later, the Devils made their first road trip to Detroit, where Bob Probert anxiously awaited a rematch with the man who had humbled him back in October. When asked about Crowder, he immediately referred to the Kimble incident. "I've got nothing to prove," said Probert. "He does. I hear he lost his last fight, to Quebec's Darin Kimble."

Crowder maintained his air of calm, though one had to wonder if he was thinking about the rematch, having just lost to a relative unknown. In typical low-key fashion, he would only say, "More than likely, it will happen."

A sellout crowd of 19,874 turned out in expectation of the fight. One enterprising fan sold T-shirts hailing the return bout. The Detroit *News* ran a "tale of the tape" article detailing the height, weight, and fight records of the combatants.

At 4:39 of the second period, Probert and Crowder shared the ice for the first time. From the bench, several Devils yelled for Crowder to come off the ice, since he was nearing the end of a shift and Probert was fresh. Crowder stayed on. After a brief discussion in which Probert said, "We have to go, they expect it," the two men dropped their gloves.

Crowder landed several hard rights early on, but the veteran Probert absorbed the blows, waited out his opponent, and erupted late in the fight. Crowder went to the ice, though whether he simply lost his footing, as he claimed, or was knocked down would remain a question.

At 11:56 of the same period, Crowder came off the bench and rushed Probert, smothering him with lefts and rights. Probert lost his jersey but again finished strongly, throwing Crowder to his knees.

After the game Crowder refused to discuss the fights, claiming that there had already been too much hype. "If I talk about it, it'll go on for another month," he said. "So, no comment."

Crowder's difficulties as a full-time player late in the season seemed to mirror the problems of his team. Both appeared to suffer from a lack of focus and intensity. His tranquil, leave-me-alone-and-I'll-leave-you-alone attitude was reflected in all aspects of his game. Despite being a member of the checking line with Boschman and Pat Conacher, the large right wing rarely played to his size, refusing to instigate punishing physical play just as he would not instigate fights.

If any indication was needed to demonstrate Crowder's diminished presence, two of his rare late-season fights would suffice. An unimpressive decision over Jay Caufield of Pittsburgh and a draw with old nemesis John Kordic of Washington (they originally had fought during Crowder's brief 1989–90 stint) revealed a less formidable Crowder, even against unspectacular opponents. Caufield is not even ranked because of his clumsiness, and Kordic would leave the Caps shortly afterwards due to an alcohol problem.

On March 3 coach Cunniff was fired following a tirade after a 3–1 loss to Boston. Crowder's patient mentor was gone, replaced by Tom McVie, who promised immediately that players who didn't produce wouldn't play. Crowder was benched during the third period of a March 13 win over Toronto, in which he made several bad passes early in the game, obviously due to poor concentration.

There was nowhere to go but down for Crowder, who was scratched from several games before completely yielding his spot to various players, including Jamie Huscroft. Despite minuscule contributions, Huscroft started in Crowder's spot throughout the playoff series with Pittsburgh, which went seven games before the Devils were eliminated. Unlike Crowder, Huscroft would freely instigate and provoke the opposition, which endeared him to McVie despite his tendency to take harmful penalties.

By the time the Devils dispersed at season's end, Crowder had executed a 180-degree turn from his early-season position of prominence. Reporters covering the Devils freely predicted that he would be trade bait during the off-season. His only hope for remaining with the team was rooted in the possibility that his nemesis, McVie, would be replaced.

What did the Crowder experiment in 1990–91 prove?

Several things. To begin with, his early fights demonstrated that a player with modest talents can become a headliner if he wins enough fights with enough tough opponents in a short time. Secondly, Crowder proved early in the season that if he was aligned with the "right" linemates he could be an asset to his team.

For a time, early in the season, Troy appeared capable of improving to the competency level of a Probert. Crowder worked well with Boschman and Stewart and at one point in late fall looked good enough to be a regular. There was, however, one major problem: unlike Probert, Rick Tocchet, and other tough guys who have made it big, Crowder seemed to lack the inner fire that would compensate for his natural deficiencies. In short, he was simply too laid-back to be effective over the long haul. This was obvious from his regular turns as a forward. With more vigorous use of his body as a checking forward, Crowder could have intimidated the foe in a legal (by hockey standards) way.

Whether Crowder's 1990–91 ending would have been different had

Cunniff remained coach is a moot point. Troy appeared to lose his zest long before Cunniff was gone. During the summer free agent Crowder was claimed by the Red Wings and was given a $350,000 contract. If he decides he wants to work on all facets of his game, the possibility remains that he could be as useful as he had been in the early stages of 1990–91. If not, he will merely be another big guy remembered for winning a couple of fights before moving into NHL obscurity.

POSTSCRIPT: THE NHL'S VIEW OF FIGHTING

Fighting has been the bane of the NHL presidency dating back to the administration of the league's first president, Frank Calder. A former newspaper man, it was Calder who suspended Boston's Eddie Shore for nearly killing Toronto's Ace Bailey during a game at Boston Garden.

Nevertheless, Calder was reasonably tolerant of fighting, considering it an intrinsic aspect of hockey. His successor, Mervyn "Red" Dutton, shared the same understanding view of hockey bad guys — and well he should. During his lengthy NHL career as a defenseman with the Montreal Maroons and New York Americans, Dutton constantly was involved in fights and therefore showed no inclination toward severity in dealing with roughhouse players. When Dutton left the president's office for Clarence Campbell, the essential policy toward fighting was maintained. Yes, there would be the usual five-minute majors, match, and misconduct penalties but Campbell, a former referee, shared the same feeling of tolerance as Dutton and Calder.

It should be noted that Calder and Dutton operated in the pretelevision era and that Campbell was president for many years before video replay began depicting fights in their gory detail. By the time John Ziegler became president in 1977 the view toward fighting had changed dramatically. An era of goon hockey had been spawned by the Boston Bruins and Philadelphia Flyers and, for the first time in the sport's history, hockey was being widely criticized for excessive fighting.

The antiviolence bloc has remained vocal through the 1990s and has had such spokesmen as superstar Wayne Gretzky, who went out of his way to condemn fighting in his autobiography published in 1990. In it Gretzky noted:

> *Hockey is the only team sport in the world that actually encourages fighting. I have no idea why we let it go on. The game itself is so fast, so exciting, so much fun to watch, why do we have to turn the ice red so often? Why do the best shots in a game have to be on somebody's nose instead of somebody's net?*
>
> *Figure this one out: You can accidentally high-stick a guy and get thrown out of a game, but two guys can stand there and beat each other dizzy and not be thrown out of the game. What sense does that make? In fact, they can stand there and beat each other to a pulp twice in a game and not be thrown out.*

Ziegler and company have been hypersensitive — and consummately defensive — about the fighting issue. His administration succeeded in eliminating bench-clearing brawls but never moved to banish fisticuffs. Ziegler made his position clear during an interview:

> *You can't eliminate fighting. That's a fiction. Basketball hasn't eliminated fighting, football hasn't, baseball hasn't. Whether we should punish more severely people who fight with each other is a legitimate question. I certainly don't think that it is the principal part of our entertainment. By the same token, I think that if you immediately suspended everybody who took a swing at somebody then you would alter the game substantially. Going out and provoking somebody would be a tactic to get them out of the game. I would send somebody out who would be in front of a hometown crowd of the star of the home team and get him so embarrassed that he would have no other reaction than to stand up and take a swing at him. And as soon as he does it, he's out of the game.*

The league's contention is that fighting in hockey is grossly exaggerated by the media. NHL officials cite a broadcaster such as New York's Warner Wolf, who on the one hand condemns fighting and on the other unfailingly shows fights in what television producers like to call "short bites" on their broadcasts.

"We can't control that," says Ziegler. "We can't go to NBC or CBS or their affiliates and say, 'Just show goals, don't show any of the other stuff,' because as long as we have that in the game, they're entitled to show it. And even though it might not be representative of the 60 minutes that is out there, they have the privilege to show that."

Violence in Hockey — Where Does It Go from Here?

One of the most damaging statements ever made about the game of hockey was uttered in complete jest by the humourist Rodney Dangerfield, who once observed, "I went to a fight, and a hockey game broke out."

Although fighting generally plays a minimal part in any given NHL game, it has become eternally associated with the sport, and in a most negative way.

As noted earlier, the criticism began mushrooming in the late 1960s, growing in intensity during the era of Philadelphia's Broad Street Bullies. The term *goon* became an integral part of hockey parlance, alongside poke-check, slapshot, and offside.

For the most part, the ice barons have been extremely defensive about the critiques. "Look at baseball," they would say. "There are fights on the ball field. Look at football players; they're much more violent than we are."

While there was a certain logic to this defensive stance, the fact remained that, for better or worse, pro hockey had been stuck with a brawling image that would bring it diminishing returns in the marketplace.

By the late 1980s, it was not uncommon for a fight-filled NHL game to be characterized as "Wrestlemania on ice."

In time, some prominent hockey personalities, led by Wayne Gretzky, campaigned for a curb on — if not the complete elimination of — fighting.

The NHL took notice and instituted modest reforms, but nothing nearly as stringent as a ban on fighting. And the beatings went on. Thus the 1990–91 season featured a season-long heavyweight championship challenge between Bob Probert and Troy Crowder, and a well-publicized and successful quest by the Rangers to obtain supergoon Joe Kocur, not to mention riotous behaviour between the Blackhawks–Blues and Flames–Kings in the final weeks of the regular season.

The NHL's attempts to minimize its World Wrestling Federation caricature was not helped in March 1991 when Los Angeles coach Tom Webster and Calgary's Doug Gilmour slugged it out at the Flames bench. The criticism heard then was simply a rehash of the knocks heard over and over again from critics across the spectrum. Jeff Gordon of the St. Louis *Post-Dispatch* succinctly noted, "The National Hockey League is sooooo defensive about its image as a World Wrestling Federation for skaters, yet it tolerates the sort of silly antics that occurred between the arch rival Kings and Flames."

Confronted by such verbal assaults, the league has conducted studies to determine how the public views hockey fighting.

"The conclusion we got," reveals a highly placed NHL official, "is that the average fan accepts an ordinary fight that erupts spontaneously in the heat of the game. But he and she disapprove of the gratuitous goonery for the sake of goonery."

In essence, the NHL remains in the same quandary that it found itself in ten years ago; it recognizes that it has a black eye from fighting, but it remains convinced that fighting should not be totally banned from the game.

The prospects for any meaningful change are minimal in the years to come. There are two reasons for this. The first is that continued expansion and the creation of new pro leagues will thin the ranks of talented players so egregiously that goons will proliferate as they did in the late 1960s and early 1970s, when the NHL underwent its vast expansion. And the second is that too many team owners are fearful that attendance would drop if fighting were abolished. Hence, they opt for the status quo.

So the likelihood is that the hockey you see today, with minor modifications, will be the tough hockey you see in 1999, give or take a few goons.